Henry William Pullen

Handbook of Ancient Roman Marbles

Or, a History and Description of all Ancient Columns and Surface Marbles...

Henry William Pullen

Handbook of Ancient Roman Marbles
Or, a History and Description of all Ancient Columns and Surface Marbles...

ISBN/EAN: 9783744773386

Printed in Europe, USA, Canada, Australia, Japan

Cover: Foto ©Thomas Meinert / pixelio.de

More available books at **www.hansebooks.com**

HANDBOOK
OF
ANCIENT ROMAN MARBLES

ABERDEEN UNIVERSITY PRESS.

HANDBOOK

OF

ANCIENT ROMAN MARBLES

OR

A HISTORY AND DESCRIPTION OF ALL ANCIENT COLUMNS AND SURFACE MARBLES STILL EXISTING IN ROME, WITH A LIST OF THE BUILDINGS IN WHICH THEY ARE FOUND

By the Rev. H. W. PULLEN, M.A.

FORMERLY CHAPLAIN OF H.M. ARCTIC SHIP "ALERT," AUTHOR OF "THE FIGHT AT DAME EUROPA'S SCHOOL," ETC.

LONDON
JOHN MURRAY, ALBEMARLE STREET
1894

ANCIENT ROMAN MARBLES.

Part I.

INTRODUCTION.

The following little treatise does not pretend to be scientific, or complete, or classical. It merely deals with an interesting subject from a picturesque, historical, and (most especially) a local point of view. The study of marbles, as such, would occupy a life-time, and require an efficient training in the principles of geology, mineralogy, and chemistry. I have done little more than give a list, with approximately accurate names, of the few hundred species which are found in the churches and galleries of Rome; and which invite the attention of the English visitor, first, because they are beautiful; secondly, because of their historical associations; and, thirdly, because they are confined within the space of a few square miles, and may be leisurely examined in the course of an ordinary season.

On the other hand, while disclaiming all pretence of scientific research, it has been my endeavour to make out a good case for the dignity and worthiness of the pursuit itself. It would appear to be pretty generally assumed that the study of marbles is a more or less childish diversion, which may be harmlessly taken up by young persons in search of something pretty and attractive, but which lies absolutely outside the limits of the legitimate antiquities of Rome. Students of archæology must surely, however, be well aware that there does not exist a single slab, or column, or tiniest fragment of ancient marble in any church or gallery or workshop in Rome, which was not brought there expressly at fabulous expense, and at the cost of infinite labour, by the very same old Romans who built the Palaces of the Caesars, and the Baths of Caracalla, and the Colosseum. Under the rule of the Emperors, Rome was a city of marble. Every public building, and every private mansion of any pretension to luxury or elegance, glistened with marble, inside and without. Columns and surface walls and statues shone everywhere like polished mirrors; and, except in the case of wall-painting and mosaic pavement, no other method of decoration was known. And all this would have concerned but little the point for which I am now contending, if Rome had been a marble city merely because the Alban hills were marble mountains, and the Campagna a marble plain. The sumptuous embellishment of temples, baths, and patrician villas with costly marbles would then have been the most natural thing in the world, the material being close at hand. It surprises nobody to find brick buildings in a brick country, granite buildings in a granite country, and wooden buildings in a forest country, where there is neither brick nor stone. But, as a matter of fact, there was no marble anywhere near Rome. The surrounding district was purely volcanic, and furnished little else except *travertine*, *tufa* and *peperino;* so that the wholesale employment of marble on so vast a scale proves, first, a deliberate intention to beautify the city at any cost, and, secondly, a deliberate choice of this particular substance as the best means of doing so. Surely, when Emperors and Consuls went absolutely wild over the importation from far distant lands of the rarest and loveliest marbles for the adornment of their buildings, they then and there stamped upon marble decoration, as such, the impress of Roman antiquity, and secured for ever to slab and plinth and column the self-same dignity which invests the most imposing ruins of ancient Rome. It is not the fault of the marble that being costly, and a tempting object to greedy eyes, it has been stripped from off the walls, and the long thin lines of narrow bricks laid bare. And yet the bricks get all the credit of the antiquity, though the glittering panel of black *lumachella* with curly white snails, which once faced their pilasters, lay in process of formation at the bottom of some Egyptian sea millions of years before Rome or Athens or even Nineveh was heard of. However, I am not now insisting upon the geological antiquity of the stone, which nobody would dispute; though it does seem a little hard that marbles should virtually be denied a place among the legitimate antiquities of Rome, while as a matter of fact they are co-eval both in design and execution with the oldest monuments one could name, except the *peperino* and *tufa* walls, and, of course, immeasurably older even than these as regards their original construction.

To the thoughtful student of Roman history, whether classical or Christian, the investigation of ancient marbles is equally important and attractive. No reference either to the political, religious, or private life, of the wonderful people whose footprints we love to trace out along an interminable Sacred Way can be complete without it. It is impossible to exaggerate the affection which they entertained for marbles. After a conquest in time of war, the columns brought home from foreign temples and theatres were esteemed among the choicest of the spoil. In time of peace, when the rulers of the city could find nothing better for idle hands to do than persecute the heretics of the age, many thousands of Christians were condemned to labour in the quarries of Asia Minor or one of the Greek Islands, that the supply of marble should not fail. And this circumstance invests our subject with a positively sacred interest; because it is nothing less than certain, that out of the 6000 columns now existing in Rome, many hundreds, at least, must have been excavated and fashioned into shape, and carved and polished, by a noble army of confessors, who had given up their goods, their liberty, and their homes, to keep our infant faith alive. We possess, unfortunately, no record of the amount of marble actually imported; but some idea of its stupendous quantity may be gathered from the consideration that, although for upwards of a thousand years such treasures were in course of wholesale destruction by earthquake, inundation, and fire; though columns without number were carried off or overthrown by barbarian conquerors as the Empire slowly fell; though huge blocks and capitals and friezes were powdered into dust by bricklayers and burnt into quicklime; though probably not a hundredth part of her treasures yet remains—Rome is still the richest marble city in the world. One of the most flourishing of native industries is that of the stone-cutter (*scarpellino*), who polishes and fits into table-tops, or carves into fanciful ornaments, the scraps which he finds in well-known hunting grounds; and although such relics are far less plentiful than formerly, those who know where to look may always be sure that an afternoon spent in diligent search will yield quite as many fragments of marble as can be conveniently carried home. Surely it is almost inconceivable that among all the learned writers who have so cleverly piloted the British tourist through this delightful labyrinth of temples, and palaces, and tombs, not one should ever have devoted more than a scanty page to some half a dozen perhaps out of the 150 well-defined species of marble which adorn the ancient buildings of Consular and Imperial Rome. All other arts and sciences, or (if these words should sound too big) all other hobbies, which any one may please to take up for purposes of amusement or instruction, have their pocket hand-books and elementary treatises. Every conceivable branch of natural history has been amply illustrated. There are popular works on astronomy, geology, electricity, and every science under the sun; while the art student may wander through Picture Galleries and Museums of Sculpture with some pleasantly written little volume in his hand, helping him to observe what is best worth observing, and teaching him the principles upon which a correct taste may be formed. But scarcely anything has ever been done for the student of ancient marbles. Not one single book on the subject exists in English, and it is just half a century since any such work was published in Italian. This treatise was compiled by a Roman lawyer named Corsi, and may be bought unbound at any Italian bookseller's in the city for four francs. It gives a history of the importation of marbles to the city, a description of the various species, and a complete list of all the ancient columns in every church and other building in Rome†—though in this respect the book is now a little out of date, many of the columns existing in Corsi's time having been

---

† Delle Pietre Antiche; *Trattato di Faustino Corsi*, Romano, ed. 3, Roma, 1845.

removed or even destroyed during the process of street improvement. The list is also unsatisfactory to this extent, that it includes for the most part columns only, giving but few illustrations of surface ornament; so that unless the marble was of a kind which is quarried in large blocks or shafts, of sufficient size to be used for columns, Corsi will seldom help the tourist to find an example of it—and, of course, many of the most beautiful and precious marbles can only be obtained in small pieces, available for slabs a few feet square at the most, or for plinths, narrow bands and fillets, a holy water basin, or the tabernacle upon an altar. In 1825 Corsi completed a fine collection of 1000 specimens, in tablets about five inches by three and a half, and published a catalogue of their names. Two years later he sold his collection to the **University of Oxford**, where it yet remains; and some time afterwards disposed of a second set of slabs, smaller in size, to a purchaser in London, from whom they passed eventually to the **Geological Museum** in Jermyn Street. These two collections, though of the highest value and interest, are of little practical use to English students. Oxford lies a good deal out of the way; while the specimens in Jermyn Street have been arranged for want of space in such a position and in so bad a light that it is quite impossible to examine them thoroughly. About the year 1830, the brothers *Tommaso* and *Francesco Belli*, both Roman lawyers, got together two splendid collections, and published thereof a descriptive catalogue which may now and then be picked up at a bookstall, but is very rare. One of these sets, amounting to 600 oblong specimens, is now in the **University** of the Sapienza; the other was bought by the late Cardinal Antonelli, and has, I believe, been dispersed. The former collection, now much neglected, was bought for the University by the reigning Pontiff for 6000 scudi (2*l.* a slab). The same institution possesses also a set of smaller square specimens (about 1000), acquired by Prof. Sanguinetti, and admirably arranged by Prof. Romolo Meli, when Director of the Geological Museum. But the most important collection of all for purposes of study, especially to an English traveller, is that of *M. Ravestein*, for many years Belgian minister at the Vatican. This gentleman collected 764 examples, which were arranged and catalogued by Belli, and afterwards presented by their owner, together with numerous Etruscan, Egyptian, and miscellaneous antiquities, to the museum of the PORTE DE HAL at **Brussels**. The whole of the upper floor of this interesting building has been assigned to M. Ravestein's various contributions, of which an excellent catalogue, extending to nearly 700 pages, may be purchased on the spot for a franc; and no better way of studying ancient marbles can be suggested to the British tourist than a visit to Brussels on his way to Rome, and two or three long mornings in the Ravestein Museum, catalogue in hand.

The three great European centres of ancient marbles are **Rome, Venice,** and **Ravenna.** The wonderful Mosque at *Cordova* enjoyed formerly the reputation of making a fourth; but it has been ascertained that among its 800 or 900 columns only twenty at the most were brought from Africa or the East, the remainder being entirely from local quarries. We are not now concerned with Venice or Ravenna; but I may observe that after a winter spent in studying the marbles of Rome, a visit to either of those cities will be found doubly interesting—first, because a multitude of old friends with new faces will at once be recognised, and, secondly, because the close connection of the Venetians with Constantinople, under the Byzantine rule, gave them facilities for the importation in considerable abundance of species which are extremely rare in Rome. Columns and surface marbles of undoubted antiquity, derived from some Roman city on or near their site, exist also at *Naples, Capua, Palermo*, and several of the smaller provincial towns of Italy; while others have been carried off or purchased from some Roman church or gallery to adorn the Glyptothek at *Munich*, the Japanese palace at *Dresden*, the corridors of the Louvre in *Paris*, and even the South Kensington Museum. *Pisa* imported a few columns from the East; but her convenient proximity to the Carrara Mountains, where marbles of great beauty and variety are quarried in abundance, leads to the suspicion that most of her so-called

Oriental marbles are local. The Mosques of *Constantinople* and *Tunis*, and several old basilicas in Palestine, are unsurpassed for the magnificence of their columns; but these treasure-houses are either closed to the tourist altogether, or are shown upon such conditions as to render any careful examination of material out of the question.

The method of transport to Rome has been recorded by Pliny and other classical historians, and is interesting. The superintendent of works at the quarry placed upon each column the year in which it was excavated, the name of the Consul or Emperor, and a number corresponding to that in the bill of lading. The columns were then shipped in vessels of peculiar form, manned sometimes by 200 or 300 rowers, and conveyed to Porto, at the mouth of the Tiber. Here they were transferred to flat-bottomed boats resembling rafts, and piloted up the river to a quay specially constructed for receiving them, just under the crest of the Aventine, at the precise spot where the tramway now turns abruptly away from the Tiber towards the Pyramid of Cestius and S. Paolo. From the purpose to which it was exclusively applied, this quay was called the MARMORATA, by which name the adjacent river-bank is still known. This point was conveniently situated for the transport of large blocks and monoliths to the Palatine Hill or the Forum, and it is probable that the stone-cutters of ancient times had their workshops close by; but the *Scarpellini* of mediæval days settled themselves bodily between the Chiesa Nuova and the Church of S. Apollinare, where they occupied an extensive and populous quarter. For their convenience another wharf was constructed about 175 yards above the Ponte S. Angelo, remains of which were discovered in 1891.

A few words must needs be said upon the unavoidably dry subject of definition and classification. Correctly speaking, marble is some variety of carbonate of lime; and the name was originally applied only to the white or statuary marbles, such as Parian, Pentelic, or Carrara—called by the Romans *Marmor Lunense*, because shipped from the port of Luna. True marble burns into quick-lime—a use, alas! to which the degenerate Romans of the post-classical age very generally applied it for making mortar; and it usually effervesces when solved by means of acids in water. Many species indeed, externally much alike, and disfigured by dirt or exposure to the air, can only be determined by chemical experiments, such as the application to their surface of various testing fluids and acids. For purposes of commerce, however, the name of marble is applied by stone-cutters and builders to ANY HARD STONE WHICH IS CAPABLE OF RECEIVING A FINE POLISH; and in this sense the stones employed in ancient Roman buildings may be divided into fifteen groups —it being understood that the classification is purely arbitrary, and is adopted for the sake of its practical convenience rather than for its scientific accuracy.

I. **White** or **Statuary marbles,** which are either uniformly white in various shades, or white streaked with grey.

II. **Black** or **grey marbles.**

III. **Coloured marbles,** comprising only yellow and red.

IV. **Veined** or **variegated marbles,** of almost every hue.

V. **Shell marbles,** containing molluscous animals, and formed for the most part at the bottom of prehistoric seas.

VI. **Breccia,** which is a conglomerate of angular stones or rounded pebbles, cemented together by a paste of gravel or clay.

VII. **Affricano,** belonging properly to the last named group, but presenting well-defined characteristics of its own.

VIII. **Alabasters,** which according to the ancient Roman signification of the word are simply stalagmites, formed by the dropping of water, charged with carbonate of lime, in stalactitic caves. (Modern alabaster, found in perfection near Volterra, is a compact variety of sulphate of lime.)

IX. **Jaspers, Agates,** and **precious stones.**

X. **Arenaceous** and **calcareous stones.**

XI. **Serpentine,** of which the well-known *Verde antico* is the finest example.

XII. **Porphyry,** which may be either red, black, grey, or green. It consists chiefly of feldspar, coloured by tiny particles of copper or iron.

XIII. **Granite,** a combination of mica, quartz, and feldspar.

XIV. **Basalt,** a species of compressed lava, almost as hard as bronze.

XV. **Travertine** and **Volcanic stones.**

A large proportion of the Italian names are merely descriptive of the nature or colour of the marble—such as *Breccia*, which can mean nothing in the world but 'breach'; and *Verde antico*, which to an Italian ear is simply 'ancient green'. To the English student, however, such names are highly convenient, as they not only describe the material at once to those who choose to translate them in their own minds, but answer the second purpose of a picturesque and *bonâ fide* name to those who accept them as they stand. It would sound strange and weak to an Englishman to hear a marble called 'ancient green'; whereas *Verde antico* satisfies his ear at once, though, of course, he is perfectly well aware that it means precisely the same thing. The French have translated *Verde antico* into *Vert antique*, and this name has unfortunately been too generally received in England. It is mischievous in two ways—first, as conveying an impression that the marble is French, which it is not in any sense whatever; and, secondly, as being far less natural and less easy of pronunciation to an Englishman than the simple *Verde antico*. In proof of this, you may often see in English books the combination *Verde antique*, or *Verd antique*,† which, as far as I know, is neither French, nor English, nor Italian. It is much better to leave the Italian words alone, and let them serve the double office of descriptive and proper names.

I. The most easily recognised among our first group of marbles is the species quarried at Mount Hymettus, close to Athens, with its straight parallel lines of bluish grey running throughout the entire length of a block or shaft. It was much employed for Pagan and early Christian sarcophagi. The finest examples in Rome are the wonderful columns at *S. Pietro in Vincoli* and *S. Maria Maggiore*, which the canons on high festivals, by way of making their church look as splendid as possible, cover up with red calico at a penny half-penny a yard, hiding what is perhaps the most magnificent feature of the building—a striking instance of the estimation in which marbles are held, even in the very head-quarters of their splendour. Most travellers, and almost all the guide books, mistake this **Marmo Imezio,** as the Italians call it, for *cipollino;* which never displays perfectly straight lines or stripes for any considerable length, but is always more or less wavy or zigzag, and very generally has a tendency to green. One of the most inter-

---

† The marble is thus nick-named in the official guide to the Museum of Practical Geology.

esting of the statuary marbles is **Marmo Tirio**, from Mount Lebanon, near the ancient Tyre. The steps of the *Scala Santa* are made of it, as well as several statues in the Vatican and Capitoline Museums. It may be recognised by its bluish hue, and by its dense crowd of little bubbles or globules, which give it exactly the appearance of boiled sago.

II. **Bigio antico** is very common in Rome, there being more columns of this material than of any other, except grey granite. It is not a striking marble as a rule, though some of its varieties are of extreme beauty. Among the best are the pillars which divide the compartments of the *Galleria dei Candelabri* at the Vatican, and the twelve exquisitely fluted Doric columns in the Chapel of St. Benedict at *S. Paolo*, which were brought from Veii. To this group belongs **Bianco e Nero antico**, of which the four shafts at the baldacchino of *S. Cecilia* are generally considered the finest specimens. It may be distinguished from inferior and modern species, similar in colour, by the triangular disposition of its markings, and by the coating of grey dust which covers its black portions. There are two lovely and very typical little columns in the Sacristy of *S. Ignazio*.

Bianco e Nero tigrato is evenly marked with small pools of black and white, flushed with pink. There is a good deal of it at the *Villa Borghese*. The scarpellini call it *Granito di Santa Prassede*, because the slab on which the saint slept, still preserved at her church on the Esquiline, is made of it. But it is not a granite at all; and the student will do well never to accept the names assigned to marbles by the scarpellini, as they are generally mere nick-names, wholly unscientific, and of no use whatever for purposes of identification. The same caution should be observed in reading any book, or extract from any book, which treats our subject from a builder's or house-decorator's point of view; because it is certain to be utterly valueless the moment it touches the marbles of ancient Rome. In such a book, of which I forget the title, the author goes into fits of rapture over the magnificence of the grouped *cipollino* columns which adorn the Church of *S. Maria sopra Minerva* —every scrap of which, above a man's height from the ground, is painted in imitation (*scagliola*, as the Italians call it), and not marble at all. This **scagliola**, which is a composition of marble dust cemented with plaster of Paris and glue, is a favourite method of cheap decoration in these economical days, and is sometimes—especially in Italy—so cleverly done as to be extremely deceptive. One of the worst examples of its use in Rome may be observed on the walls of the staircase which ascends on the right to the *Cortile di S. Damaso* at the foot of the Scala Regia. One of the best is at the aforesaid Church of the Minerva; where, however, anybody who compares the upper part of the pillars with the lower, in a moderately good light, will soon detect the points of difference, and is not likely to be deceived again. The large columns in *S. M. dell' Orazione* offer a clever imitation of *Porfido bigio*.

Another cheap device, almost as reprehensible as scagliola, is **impellicciatura**—literally 'furring up,' or muffling up in fur. This term is applied in Italy to pillars of brick or stone, overlaid with thin strips or irregular patches of marble, like the gaudy red jasper columns at *S. M. in Via Lata* and *S. Marco*. Even the great Corsi was taken in by this abominable trick, and described the four large columns of *Fiore di Persico* in the right transept of *S. Carlo al Corso* as entire. If they were so, they would be of fabulous value; but anybody who pleases to look at them may see by the suspicious regularity of the pattern, and uniformity of the hue, that the whole surface of the shaft is simply veneered.

III. The well-known **Giallo antico** comprises endless varieties of shade and colour, and is of surpassing beauty. The Romans called it Numidian marble, but it probably came from a mountain range between Algiers and Oran, where quarries of the same species still exist. The columns at the *Arch of Constantine* are made of it—except the one at the corner nearest the Meta Sudans, which is of Carrara. It is, however, never seen to advantage, when it has lost its polish by exposure to dust and rain. At a tomb in *S. Francesca Romana* are two very singular columns of this marble, broadly streaked with alabaster. Under the influence of fire the yellow turns almost red, as in a door frame at *S. Cecilia.*

Rosso antico is more commonly employed for statues, shallow vases, and tripods, than for columns; though there are two very large ones at the *Casino Rospigliosi*, plentifully veined with white, and half buried in a partition wall. Some fine altar steps of this material may be seen at *S. Prassede*, which Napoleon ordered off to Paris—an act of spoliation which was happily not effected. The colour is easily imitated in *terra cotta;* but a careful examination of the substance betrays the attempted fraud. The marble is always more or less minutely mottled, or streaked with hair lines of a darker shade. When broadly veined with white, it very nearly approaches *Cipollino rosso*, as in the restored parts of the Faun (Capitoline Museum). Until quite lately its quarries were unknown; but they have now been rediscovered on a promontory in the Peloponnesus, which bears the modern name of Cape Matapan; and, but for the expense of shipping it, the marble might soon be very common. **Nero antico**, which is seldom found of a pure unveined black, comes from the same promontory.

IV. Of the variegated marbles the most abundant in Rome, though it is almost unknown elsewhere, is **Porta Santa,** so called because the door-jambs of the Jubilee Gate under the portico of St. Peter's and the other great Basilicas are made of it. This marble never presents primary colours, but always shades;

and, although infinite in its varieties, it can never be mistaken for any other. It has one unfailing characteristic—a most remarkable resemblance to cold roast beef—a peculiarity so constant as to ensure its recognition at a glance. The basins of the two end fountains in the *Piazza Navona*, and of that in the *Piazza Colonna*, are faced entirely with this marble; and include, at some point or other of so large a surface, almost every known variety. A bath in the Octagon Court at the Vatican is made of a most beautifully reticulated block of *Porta Santa*, entirely different from the typical examples; and yet, if you look closely into it, the texture of cold roast beef will at once betray the nature of the marble.

Cipollino is so called from the resemblance of its veining to the vertical section of an onion (*cipolla*). These veins are of mica, and the marble will split along the lines of their strata, just as an onion will come to pieces flake by flake. Very fine typical examples are the bases of the pillars in *S. M. sopra Minerva*; but there are many varieties, among which may be noticed **Cipollino mandolato**, almond shaped in pattern, which is found on the ambones at *S. M. in Cosmedin* and on the chancel railings at the *Gesù*. **Cipollino rosso** is very rare in Rome, though common in Venice; and there are only five columns of it in Western Europe—two at Palermo, two at Ravenna, and one at Coutances in Normandy.

Everybody knows by sight the beautiful **Pavonaz-**

zetto or Phrygian marble, with its curious hue of clotted blood—an unpleasing simile, but an unfailing characteristic. No matter how much the colour may otherwise vary, the clotted appearance is never absent from the purple. Statues of royal Dacian prisoners are often clothed with it, and it is a favourite material for holy water basins and altar railings. Sometimes it assumes a most exquisitely delicate silvery tone, as on the pilasters of the little baptistery at *S. Marco*, or the four fluted columns at *S. Tommaso* in *Formis* —the latter a perfect marvel of beauty.

The most showy, if not the most beautiful of all the variegated marbles, is **Fiore di Persico** (peach-blossom). It is not uncommon in the form of slabs and smaller pieces, but exceedingly rare in large solid masses. There are only two columns in Rome; † but the traveller in Sicily will find six very handsome ones in the Cappella Palatina at *Palermo*.

Nearly allied to the latter in form, though different in colour, is **Cottanello,** a purely Italian marble, still quarried in the Sabine hills. It is rather coarse and common looking, of a yellowish bricky red, and it furnished most of the main columns for the Vatican Basilica. The ancient Romans appear to have excavated from quarries of a better and purer type, known as **Cottanello antico**, good examples of

---

† Two more have lately been found near S. Martino, and are lying within the rails in the Court of the Pal. dei Conservatori.

which are the spheres on the railings of the side chapels at the *Gesù.*

V. The **Shell marbles** are all extremely beautiful. Most of them are called **Lumachella**, from *lumaca* (snail). In the left transept of *S. Agostino* is a narrow fillet of black lumachella, very precious and rare; and there are four priceless slabs of a different variety on the chancel floor at *S. M. in Via Lata.*

Astracane, another fine shell marble, was formerly supposed to come from Astrakan, but is now believed to have been quarried near Agra, in India. It may be seen on the altar rails at *S. Andrea della Valle;* but the handsomest columns with which I am acquainted are in the Pal. Corsini at *Florence,* the Campo Santo at *Bologna,* and the Museum of the Prado at *Madrid.*

Broccatello comes from Tortosa in Spain, and for that reason is far more common at Naples than in Rome, having been largely imported for church ornamentation during the rule of the Spanish viceroys. The largest columns in Europe adorn the Cathedral of the Pilar, at *Zaragoza;* but there are many also in the Chapel of St. Januarius at Naples, and in other churches of that city. Only two columns exist in Rome. The predominant colour of this beautiful marble is reddish lilac or yellow, in proportion to the quantity of embedded snails; the yellow representing the molluscous animal himself—the lilac the soft sea-bed in which he sank to rest. Magnificent surface specimens of the lilac variety may be seen on the walls of the

Cappella Borghese at *S. M. Maggiore;* and equally fine ones of the yellow kind at *S. Cecilia.*

Of **Occhio di Pavone** (peacock's eye) there are two splendid columns in the *Vatican Library*, and two others at a doorway in the *University*. The eyes are simply petrified oysters, and the general hue of the marble is either reddish brown or light purple.

VI. **Breccia** of every kind is abundant, as might be expected from its geological formation. Wherever broken bits of rock have been crushed by external pressure, and cemented together by a paste, you have at once a *Breccia*. When the conglomerate is composed of rounded pebbles instead of angular fragments, it is called by the Italians *frutticolosa*, and by the English *pudding-stone*. The most beautiful of the Breccias, and perhaps the most beautiful marble in the world, is the green Egyptian, of which there are two columns in the so-called billiard-room at the *Villa Albani*, and a short pillar in the *Pal. dei Conservatori* on the Capitol. Another very lovely little shaft in the *Pal. Pitti* at Florence is habitually used by some coldblooded copyist as a post for tying up the legs of his easel—such is the respect paid to rare and precious marbles by artists and directors of Museums. Several exquisite columns of this marble were carried off by Napoleon to Paris, where they now adorn the corridors of the Louvre; but the two finest of all, as far as I am able to judge, are in the Church of *S. Francesco di Paola* at Naples.

Another handsome species, which, like the *Breccia verde di Egitto*, partakes of the nature of a pudding-stone, is **Breccia traccagnina**, so called from an old Italian name for the costume of a harlequin. It much resembles a kind of brawn or galantina of various cold meats, plentifully sprinkled with truffles. These similes are not very refined; but marbles have a way of suggesting comparisons homely and prosaic, rather than romantic and poetical. There are two very remarkable columns of *Breccia traccagnina* in the Church of *S. M. in Via*.

The best known of this group is **Breccia corallina**, which varies much both in form and colour, but usually presents small angular fragments of delicate pink, as at the baldacchino of *S. Croce*. Any large surface of this marble is frequently found in alternate patches of breccia and uniform masses of flushed pink, veined with rose—a pointed illustration of the little value which can be placed upon the tiny specimens with which collectors are mostly contented. Porphyries, Serpentines, Granites, and tolerably crowded examples of Lumachella, may be recognised at once, be the surface ever so small; while a dozen well-defined species of Breccia, Affricano, Alabaster, or some variegated marble, might be chipped off, in morsels a couple of inches long, from the same square foot of a panel. For which reason collectors are advised to have nothing to do with table-tops, but to carry home as a souvenir of their visit to Rome a slab or fragment of such dimensions that at least it can be confidently named.

Breccia di Settebasi is tolerably plentiful, and may be distinguished by its small oblong markings, which always run in one direction like a stream. It derives its name from Septimius Bassus, who had a Villa sumptuously adorned with this marble at the miscalled *Roma Vecchia*, on the *Via Tuscolana*. Its general hue is greyish violet, but it is often beautifully flushed with blood-red or golden yellow. Akin to it, but of a very minute pattern, is **Breccia a Semesanto**, known at once by its being splashed all over against the grain with chips of chalky white, which look exactly like fresh paint. It is so called from its resemblance to a paste of sugar-plums, having the form of seeds. † **Breccia Quintilina**, found sparingly at Hadrian's Villa, and much employed in the decorations of the Villa Quintiliorum, on the Appian Way, has pebbles of tortoise-shell embedded in orange and dark grey, and is generally considered the rarest and most beautiful of all.

VII. **Marmo Affricano** is strictly speaking a *Breccia*, and is the only coloured marble which contains any black. To this peculiarity it owes its name, for it has nothing to do with Africa, but comes from

---

† Such is Corsi's derivation; but the word may possibly be derived from *Semo Sancus*, a Sabine divinity, to whom statues may have been raised in this material.

one of the Greek Islands. The colours are always vivid, and there is generally a certain amount of pink or red. Not unfrequently the whole surface is tinged with an exquisitely delicate hue of grey or green. The handsomest columns in Rome are at *S. M. dell'Orto* and *S. Giacomo al Corso:* but one of the choicest varieties, jewelled with brilliant red, may be seen on the pedestals of some busts in the entrance room of the *Villa Borghese.*

VIII. In speaking of the **Alabasters** it is necessary to observe that the modern alabaster of commerce is a totally different substance from that employed in Roman decoration. True alabaster is a fine massive or crystalline variety of gypsum, and is found in its greatest purity in the neighbourhood of *Volterra.* It is waxy in texture, and too soft to take a high polish like marble, but is chiefly used for statuettes and fancy ornaments. A similar quality, obtained from *Karnak* on the Nile, was much used by the Egyptians for cinerary urns, examples of which may be seen in the Vatican and elsewhere. ANCIENT ALABASTER, on the other hand, is a true marble, and is only found in stalactitic caves. Its formation may be thus practically, though perhaps not very scientifically, described. A drop of water, charged more or less highly with carbonate of lime, filters through the surface of the earth until it reaches the roof of a subterranean cavern, and then falls to the ground. The water gradually evaporates, leaving a deposit of carbonate of lime, which in course of ages becomes piled up into a stalagmite. As the filtration proceeds, each drop of water begins to leave behind it, before falling to the ground, first a very little, and then a very little more, of its chemical ingredients, just as the drops running down an icicle cling more and more tenaciously to their rigid spike, until the whole is frozen. In this way is formed the pendent portion of the column, or the stalactite—the two columns eventually meeting in mid-air, after the manner familiar to everybody who has visited a stalactitic cave. When no obstructions of any kind occur, the aggregate deposit of the spike will be pure white or creamy yellow; but as foreign substances, such as different kinds of earth or metals, almost invariably creep in, the layers assume every conceivable variety of form and colour.

Bearing in mind the general principle of this formation, we can almost see the process going on when we look closely into a piece of ancient alabaster. The bright colours usually indicate the admixture of some foreign mineral or metal; while the long lines or streaks, whether straight or tortuous, show the direction which each successive drop of water was forced to take, owing to some local pressure or interruption either in the upper or lower column. It is interesting to remember that **travertine,** though to all appearance as unlike alabaster as possible, is composed of precisely the same ingredients, deposited by rapidly running water in the form of a sediment at the bed of a mountain torrent, instead of being forced to trickle drop by drop into a cave.

The varieties of alabaster are infinite. M. Ravestein of Brussels enumerates 122 species; but most of them are purely fanciful, and the number may be conveniently divided by twelve. If we examine a column or any large surface of alabaster, we shall see that by cutting it up into slabs, of the usual specimen size, we may make as many varieties as we please. The genuine and constant species may be reduced to about ten: *Cotognino*, or quince-coloured; *tartaruga*, or tortoise-shell; *Sardonico*, like a bright brown sugar-candy; *pecorella* or fleecy, mottled in pink and white; *fortezzino*, with zigzag lines like the ground plan of a fortress; *Palombara*, distinguished from all others by its broad bands of opaque ivory white; *rosa*, flushed with dusky red; *erborizzato*, delicately pencilled like the foliage of a tree; *verdognolo*, of uniform transparent green; *listato*, with parallel straight or wavy lines; and *fiorito* or flowery—a general term which includes all brightly coloured species, not specially distinguished by any of the characteristics mentioned above. All these may be seen and studied at the various altars of *S. M. della Vittoria*, or *S. Catarina*, two of the richest alabaster churches in Rome.

Here, however, and in other churches renowned for their surface decoration, we are constantly offended by another cheap device of the Italians, more reprehensible than even *scagliola* or *impellicciatura*—I mean their abominable practice of dividing a slab into two halves or four quarters of its original thickness, and putting up the pieces end to end against the wall, in the form of a spread eagle. It answers the purpose of covering more space, and making one slab do the work of two or four; but it is contrary to all sound principles of decoration, and cannot be too strongly condemned. In the first place, it is intensely vulgar, and vulgarity inside a church is more than commonly offensive. In the second place, it is false, for everybody knows and recognises that the marble does not shape itself into set patterns in its quarry. And, in the third place, it utterly destroys all impression of solidity. At a glance one sees that such decoration is only skin deep; whereas the aim of the builder should be, by a perfectly legitimate expedient well understood in art, so to clothe his plinths and pedestals as to make them appear like solid cubes. This odious trick has been perpetrated to excess in the newly restored transepts and chancel of St. John Lateran; and it is not too much to say that what would otherwise have been the finest piece of wall decoration in Rome, if not in Europe, has been utterly spoilt and vulgarised thereby. Perhaps the worst example of this perverted taste is to be seen on the left of the entrance at *S. Antonio dei Portoghesi*, where some veins and blotches on a slab of *Giallo antico* have been splayed into the figure of a toad.

IX. **Jasper** is a material extremely difficult to define, as it appears to depend more upon eccentric markings and violent contrasts of colour than upon any geological characteristics of its own. There is little or no ancient jasper in Rome, and the modern specimens are not generally attractive. By way of exception, we find some beautiful slabs of **Legno pietrificato** in the Cappella Borghese at *S. M. Maggiore*. True jasper is exceedingly hard; but a soft variety called **Diaspro tenero** has been brought from Sicily, of which there are some handsome columns at *SS. Domenico e Sisto*, and some facings of pilasters under the cupola of *St. Peter's*. A showy, but decidedly vulgar species of Sicilian jasper, was much employed for surface decoration in the last century at *S. Ignazio* and *S. Antonio dei Portoghese*, and for muffling up the columns at *S. M. in Via Lata* and *S. Marco*. The nobler kinds of jasper form a connecting link between marbles and precious stones, and would scarcely fall within the limits of our subject, were they not occasionally found in vases or upon altars of unusually rich design. **Agate** occupies very much the same position, but we must perforce admit it, because it occurs not unfrequently in the form of colonnettes to the *ciborio* or tabernacle over an altar. Agate has a base of chalcedony, blended with jasper, quartz, amethyst, opal, heliotrope, cornelian, and jade. Its beauty, however, chiefly depends upon the alternation of different varieties of chalcedony and jasper. It is invariably found in the cavities of igneous rocks, akin to basalt—cavities probably formed by the escape of gas or steam from the heated flint rock, and afterwards filled with silica and other substances deposited by trickling water. Pure quartz is *silica*. AMETHYST is a form of crystallised quartz, its purple colour being probably metallic. CHALCEDONY is a somewhat waxy but translucent variety of quartz, occurring chiefly in stalactitic forms —perhaps a mixture of quartz with opal, or soluble silica. JADE, or nephrite, is a silicate of magnesia and lime. These rough definitions will show that we are here trespassing upon the domain of precious stones, with which we are not concerned. The few remaining minerals of doubtful classification, examples of which are presented to us in any Roman church or gallery, will be noticed as they occur. The same remark applies to Section X., which forms a very unimportant division of our subject.

XI. Serpentine, porphyries, and granite, are not, strictly speaking, marbles, as they contain little or no carbonate of lime. **Serpentine** was called by the ancients *Ophite*, from the Greek ὄφις, a snake; and many species bear a singular resemblance to the peculiar dull green of a serpent's skin. Common or typical serpentine is of little or no value for decorative purposes, though some of its varieties are pretty, such as the small holy water basins at *S. Salvatore in Lauro*. The finest of the choice serpentines, or *Serpentine nobili*, is **Verde antico;** and the handsomest piece of Verde antico in Rome is a table slab in the *Sala degli Animali*, because of the purity of its white and green.

There is a unique column also, very difficult to see, blotched with red, in the Lower Church at *S. Clemente*. Near Susa, and elsewhere in Piedmont, a green serpentine, much resembling verde antico, is still found, and has been extensively used in modern decoration; but it may generally be distinguished by the dulness of the green and the almost total absence of white. Another of the noble serpentines is **Verde ranocchia,** named from its frog-like markings, of which the *Sala degli Animali* has several good examples; but the most curious is a dog sitting up on his haunches in the central statue room at the *Pal. dei Conservatori*.

There is a hard, compact, and remarkably heavy kind of serpentine called **Pietra nefritica** (from νεφρὸν, a kidney), having the form of a flattened sphere, or a large round loaf which did not rise properly in the baking. These were employed by the Romans as standard weights, and a quantity of them may be seen of all sizes in the Museum of the Capitol, mixed with others of white stone, marked with the number of pounds they represented, and sometimes bearing iron rings or rivets, by means of which they could be raised. Under the rule of some of the persecuting Emperors they were tied round the necks of Christians condemned to be thrown into a well; and the *Pietra nefritica* acquired from this circumstance and ever afterwards retained the honourable appellation of 'Martyr's Stone'. Those in the Museums are, of course, purely pagan; but specimens of the Martyr's Stone itself, recovered from the well, may be seen in several churches in Rome, and are always preserved with the most loving care. Occasionally they are found also in provincial towns, as, for instance, in the little round church of S. Angelo at *Perugia*, where a good example reposes in a niche, safely guarded behind an iron grating. And this reminds me to observe that one of the chief fascinations of our present study is this— that, after working for a season at the marbles of Rome, one is constantly meeting with stray and unexpected apparitions of some familiar friend in out-of-the-way districts, which light up the whole place quite magically, and bring back delicious memories of the city in which we first learnt to love them.

XII. The ancient quarries of the well-known **red porphyry** have lately been rediscovered near the banks of the Red Sea; and the quantity appears to be so abundant that we might almost pave the streets of London with it, if, like the good old Romans, we could send slaves or captive heretics to dig it out for nothing. **Black porphyry** is much more interesting. Two most lovely columns of it, plentifully sprinkled with dark grey, stand at the top of a staircase in the Vatican, overlooking the *Sala a Croce Greca*. **Porfido verde** is peppered in the same way, but the general hue is green instead of black. There are two handsome columns of this marble in the *Ara Coeli*. *Porfido bigio* is freckled in such a very suspicious manner that the Italians call it *morviglione*, which appears to be an old word for *smallpox*, or rather for the marks which smallpox leaves behind it. Two remarkably large columns may be seen at *St. Peter's*, flanking the altar of St. Gregory, near the sacristy door. At a little distance you would certainly take them for grey granite, but on close inspection the difference will be at once perceived. The ancient quarries of this marble still exist about two miles north of the Station of *La Boulerie* on the Riviera, and remain very much in the condition in which the Romans left them.

There is a subdivision of the porphyries known as **Porfido serpentino**, which may be either green, black, or grey. The common green kind is generally, but quite erroneously, called Serpentine. It is not a Serpentine at all, but a Porphyry, differing only from the typical form in having its crystals large and oblong, scattered over the surface like chips, instead of being small, round, and peppery. Of the black variety— **Porfido serpentino nero**—there is a precious little shaft at the entrance to the closed chapel at *S. Prassede*. The student will observe that *Serpentina* is a substantive, and represents the genus; while *serpentino* is an adjective, denoting a species or variety.

XIII. The most important among the ancient monuments of **granite** still existing in Rome are the Obelisks. They are all composed of Syenite, an aggregate of feldspar, quartz, and hornblende—the last named lustrous mineral having taken the place of the mica. The quarries were situated about two miles from *Syene*, the modern Assouan. Several varieties of grey and black granite are of exceeding interest and beauty. Plentiful in Rome, though almost unknown elsewhere, is the *Lapis Psaronius*, or starling-spotted granite, called by the Italians **Granito del Foro**, because it supplied all the columns for the Forum of Trajan. **Granito della Sedia**, resembling a beautiful greenish grey lichen, is so called because it forms panels for the chair of St. Peter in the Vatican Basilica. Of **Granito verde** there is an exquisite little vase in the *Villa Albani;* and another, equally precious, but of a different type, in the *Villa Borghese*. A generally received but doubtful specimen of granite is the curiously shaped Column of the Scourging at *S. Prassede*, which presents large and untidy patches of black and white, and looks as unlike a granite as possible.

XIV. **Basalt** is variously derived from βάσανος, a touchstone, and *basal*, the Ethiopian for *iron*. It is an immensely hard solidified condition of lava, and at first sight may often be mistaken for bronze. Nearly allied to it is the **Pietra di Paragone**, or touchstone for trying the precious metals, supposed to have been found in Lydia. The most celebrated examples of basalt in Rome are the urn beneath the high altar at *S. Croce*, and a large bath in the Octagon at the *Vatican* —the latter remarkably metallic in hue. The so-called specimens of Paragone in Rome are probably jet black varieties of *Nero Antico*.

XV. There remains a group of building materials which are certainly in no sense marbles, but which can scarcely be omitted from a list of the materials employed in the construction of ancient Rome. **Selce**, a species of lava approaching the basalts, but coarser in texture, was almost exclusively employed for pavements and flagstones. The *Via Sacra*, *Via Appia*, and all the great roads which led out of the city, were paved with it. Very beautiful crystals have sometimes been found in the cavities between two layers of this lava. Mention has already been made of the formation of **Travertine**, a stone familiar to all tourists in Rome as the material of the *Colosseum* and *St. Peter's*. When closely examined its structure is curious and beautiful, the fine yellow grain giving the appearance of embedded silk-worms. Some good examples may be seen on the steps and parapets above the *Piazza di Spagna;* but the formation of the stone itself may best be observed by walking up the pathway which leads near the stream from the lower to the higher *Falls at Terni*. Blocks of travertine, as Mr. Middleton has pointed out, become ruined and disfigured in course of time, when carelessly placed *on end* by the builder, instead of being laid in the position which they occupied in the river bed from whence they were hewn. The same remark might be applied to cipollino, breccia, alabaster, and various other marbles; and it is probably for this reason that the Greeks never used monoliths, but always built up their columns in drums and courses.

Tufa is composed of volcanic ashes and sand, showered out of a crater, and afterwards compressed or stratified. It varies in colour from tawny red to greyish brown, and is found either hard or comparatively soft, according to the amount of pressure it has received. All the earlier buildings of Rome were made of tufa, but were covered with a thick coating of stucco, nearly as hard as marble, by way of protection against frost and rain. The so-called Tarpeian Rock on the cliffs of the Capitol, and the Wall of Romulus on the Palatine, are early examples of the use of tufa. The best and hardest kind was quarried on the Aventine, near the Church of *S. Saba*. In the softer qualities were excavated many Catacombs and other subterranean galleries.

Peperino is similar in formation, but a good deal harder, and is always studded with black or bluish lumps of lava. It is still quarried on the northern slopes of the Alban Hills. Alternate layers of soft tufa and peperino may be seen in the walls of the so-called *Temple of Cybele* on the Palatine.

In the following list of all the well-defined species and varieties of marble still found in the churches or galleries of Rome, I have adopted in every possible case the names given by Francesco Belli and Corsi, venturing only to correct them when they were obviously mistaken. In one instance alone have I made any arbitrary change of names. Belli was fond of calling marbles after the title of the church or altar at which they were found—Serpentina di S. Salvatore, Bigio di S. Pancrazio, Porta Santa di S. Agnese, etc. Such terms, though still largely employed by the Roman *scarpellini*, are absolutely useless as a means of identifying the marble; and I have therefore substituted for them a name descriptive of the variety itself, referring, of course, to the locality where it may be seen.

Speaking generally, I have arranged my groups, with their respective *Genera* and *Species*, very much as a writer on wild flowers would arrange a Flora. This method has appeared to me upon the whole the simplest and most convenient. The multiplication both of genera and species was a necessity forced upon me by the present fragmentary condition of the marbles. In the days when Rome was a forest of rare and costly pillars—when baths and temples were panelled from floor to ceiling with Pavonazzetto, Fiore di Persico, and Alabaster—when the walls of patrician houses shone like mirrors with great slabs of Breccia, Porta Santa, and Giallo—it would have been comparatively easy to catalogue even so vast a treasury of specimens, by reason of their colossal scale. But now that only fifty kinds of ancient marble remain to us in the form of columns, while slab and pilaster and plinth have been sawn up wholesale for the minute decorations of an altar, and cut into the thinnest strips to supply the largest surface possible, the difficulty of classification is increased a hundredfold. A block of alabaster or breccia, once easily recognised by one descriptive name, has been mutilated into twelve or fifteen fragments, every one of which requires a new name of its own; and although it is not pretended that all these are genuine species, it was better to treat them as such, and to bestow upon them some specific title, than to perplex the reader from time to time with a list of varieties a, b, c and d.

Except in the case of species which are very rare indeed, the enumeration of the churches or galleries wherein they are found is not intended to be complete. In the majority of instances, I have cited only the most typical or attainable examples, to which the student may add almost as many more as he pleases. And with two exceptions only—*Porta Santa* and *Porfido rosso*—I have fixed the maximum of references under each head to twelve.

Within these groups the Churches are arranged first, in alphabetical order, after which follow the Museums and other secular buildings. In a very few instances (enclosed within brackets) I have retained a church which has been destroyed since I made my notes therein, as a historical record, and in the hope of affording a clue to the present location of the marble. For similar reasons I have given Corsi's list of the treasures in the *Palazzo Sciarra*, which I have never seen, and which are said to have been lately removed to Paris. I have also included his enumeration of certain precious stones in the Kircherian Museum, which I have not yet succeeded in identifying.

I regret exceedingly that want of space, and the necessity of providing a pocket volume, have compelled me to adopt a somewhat hieroglyphic system of abbreviations. The reader, however, even if a stranger in Rome, will soon grow accustomed to them; while any one who is even moderately well acquainted with the city will recognise immediately his old friends under a curtailed name. The official titles of Roman churches and galleries, and the descriptive names of marbles, are often so extremely long, that it would have required an additional fifty pages of letter-press to print them all in full.

And so I commend my hobby to the patience, and—I hope I may add—the enthusiasm, of the reader. I do not claim for it more dignity than is its due. I do not pretend that the study of marbles is of equal importance with the study of Classical Antiquities, or of Mediæval or Renaissance Art. But I do say that it forms a legitimate part of the study of Antiquities from the picturesque point of view, and that it ought not to be discouraged or despised. It is not a bad thing to have a little variety, even in Rome. We cannot always be strung up to the loftiest classical pitch; and the sight of a beautifully decorated altar, especially when the names and history of its marbles have become familiar to our minds, may sometimes serve as a not unpalatable refreshment, even after a lecture in the Forum. None will regret the trifling expenditure of time and labour which can turn every church in Rome, over and above its interest for the sake of higher things, into a lovely garden full of May flowers. There are dozens upon dozens of little churches in obscure out-of-the-way streets, where all the world declares that there is not a thing to be seen; but the student of marbles will find some treasure in every one of them, which he will hunt up with fresh eagerness every time he comes back to Rome. It is the old story of Eyes and No Eyes. What to the used-up man is an insufferably dismal trudge may become to the enthusiast a regular sporting tour; and I shall be more than satisfied with my work if I can awaken in any visitor to Rome the same interest in an otherwise unattractive building that a knowledge of wild flowers, or birds, or insects, imparts to an otherwise stupid country walk in spring.

PART II.

CLASSIFIED LIST OF MARBLES, WITH A REFERENCE TO THE BUILDINGS IN WHICH THEY ARE FOUND.

THE abbreviations of churches and public or private galleries will be recognised without difficulty, since they all follow strictly the alphabetical order of the full title which the church or other building bears. The only exceptions are the following, to which the omitted prefix is supplied within brackets:—

Albani, Borghese, etc. [Villa].
Altemps, Barberini, etc. [Palazzo].
Animali [Vatican].
Ara Coeli [S. M. in].
Arazzi [Vatican].
Belvedere ,,
Biga ,,
B. N. [Braccio Nuovo, Vatican].
Busts [Vatican].
Candelabri [Vatican].
Cap. [Museo Capitolino].
Cappuccini [S. M. dei].
Castigliana [Scuola].
Chiaramonti [Vatican].
Consolazione [S. M. della].

Crypt [S. Pietro].
Egypt [Vatican].
Etruscan Mus. [Vatican].
Garden [Vatican].
Inscriptions ,,
Library ,,
Masks ,,
Minerva [S. M. sopra].
Montesanto [S. M. di].
Muses [Vatican].
Octagon [Vatican].
Rotonda ,,
Sacristy [S. Pietro].
Siciliana [Scuola].
Statues [Vatican].
Terme [Museo delle].

I. WHITE OR STATUARY MARBLES.

PARIO.

MARMOR PARIUM (*Greco duro*).—From quarries on mountain flanks, in the Island of Paros. Called by some ancient writers *Lychnite*, because of its large sparkling crystals. The Pallas of Velletri (*Louvre*) and the Venus of the Medici (*Uffizi*) are celebrated examples of this marble.

Pure white; crystals flaky and transparent.
S. Cosma Trast.; S. M. del Sole.
Albani; Borghese; Cand.; Cap.; Oct.; Porticus of Octavia.

P. giallognolo (yellowish).
S. Marcello.—B. N.; Cap.

PORINO.

MARMOR PORINUM (*Grechetto duro*).—From the neighbourhood of Olympia, in the Peloponnesus.

Similar, with more compact texture and smaller grain. Very white and sparkling, but sometimes stained with orange, whence its name—πῶρος (sandstone). The only white marble which does not effervesce at the touch of nitric acid.

S. M. in Cosm.; S. Nereo; S. Salv. in Lauro.
Belvedere; Masks; Piazza Rondinini.

PENTELICO.

MARMOR PENTELICUM (*Greco fino*).—From Mount Pentelicus, between Athens and Marathon.

Pure white, with fine dust-like opaque crystals. Turns yellow after long exposure to the air. A few barely visible veins of talc sometimes cause a faint tinge of green (see *Imezio*), for which reason Belli calls this marble *Cipolla*. The Elgin marbles in the British Museum, and the whole of the Parthenon, are of *M. Pentelicum*.

S. Antonio degli Armeni ; S. Giov. Lat. ; S. M. in Domn.

Arch of Titus ; Borghese ; Campidoglio ; Cand. ; Oct. ; Papa Giulio ; Terme.

TASIO.

MARMOR THASIUM (*Greco livido*).—From the Island of Thasos, in the Ægean Sea.

White, with a bluish tinge, compact texture, and sparkling crystals.

Ara Coeli ; Cappuccini ; S. Cecilia ; Pantheon ; S. Agost. ; S. Giorgio ; S. Fr. di Paola ; S. Lor. fuori.

B. N. ; Forum of Nerva ; Lat. ; Piazza Colonna ; Pyramid of Cestius.

LESBIO.

MARMOR LESBIUM (*Greco giallognolo*).—From the Island of Lesbos (Mytilene).

Yellowish white, stained with livid ashy black; large conspicuous crystals.

Apostoli ; S. Bibiana ; S. Giorgio ; S. M. in Cosm. ; S. Onofrio.

Albani ; Animali ; B. N. ; Cap. ; Pincio.

TIRIO.

MARMOR TYRIUM (*Greco turchiniccio*).—From Mount Lebanon, near Tyre.
Bluish white, sparingly peppered with brown, and mottled like boiled sago.
S. M. in Cosm.; S. Pietro; Scala Santa.
Albani; Animali; Belvedere; Biga; Cand.; Cap.; Quir.; Stat.

LUNENSE.

MARMOR LUNENSE (*Carrara antico*).—From the Fantiscritti † quarries at Carrara.
Lunense antico.—Pure ivory white; no crystals; texture soapy, inclining to that of china.
Albani; Biga; Borghese; Cand.; Cap.; Col. of Phocas; Oct.; Pantheon; Piazza di Pietra; Temple of Castor; T. of Vespasian.

L. macchiato (modern *Carrara*).—Common; still quarried in abundance at Crestola, Zampona, Bettolia and Ravaccione among the Carrara mountains.
White, with bluish tinge and streaks of black, or black metallic spots.
Campo Santo; S. Giacomo de' Spagnuoli.
Albani; Cand.

IMEZIO.

MARMOR HYMETTIUM (*Greco rigato*).—From Mount Hymettus, close to Athens. Much employed for

---

† So called from some ancient reliefs of soldiers sculptured in the rock.

ancient sarcophagi, both Pagan and Christian. When sawn or rubbed it emits a fetid odour, whence it has been called *M. Cipolla* (Onion marble).

Bluish white, crowded with spots like sago, and banded with straight parallel lines of grey in various shades. There is sometimes an inclination to green, owing to the presence of minute veins of talc.

Imezio colonnare.—*S. M. in Cosm; S. M. Maggiore; S. Anastasia; S. Clemente; S. Giac. degli Spagnuoli; S. Martino; S. Paolo fuori; S. Pietro in Vincoli; S. Sabina.*
Arch of Sept. Severus; Arch of Titus; Janus.

I. dentellato.—Lines toothed or jagged. *S. Lor. in Borgo.*

I. fasciato schietto.—Bands very numerous, regular, and sharply defined.
S. M. Maggiore; S. Catarina da Siena. Sala Rotonda.

I. zonale.—Bands horizontal instead of vertical.
S. Pietro.

PALOMBINO.

MARMOR CORALITICUM.—From the banks of the Coralio, in Phrygia. Seldom found in large blocks, but frequent in tiny square chips upon ancient mosaic pavements.

Palombino bianco.—Ivory white, of very fine grain, without crystals. Sometimes faintly spotted with grey.
Chiesa Nuova; S. Pudenziana.—Cand.

P. bruniccio.—White, like polished earthenware, powdered with chocolate. *Egypt.*

P. eburneo (ivory). *Minerva.*

P. latteo (milky white). *Lat. Mus.*

MARMOR MEGARENSE.—From Megaris (Livadia).

P. giallognolo lumacato.—Yellowish white, with long fragments of shells. *Egypt.*

II. BLACK OR GREY MARBLES.

MARMO GRECO.

This somewhat indefinite term is applied to a few Greek marbles whose quarries are unknown, and which cannot well be classified under any one of the established groups. Some of the species very nearly approach *Marmo Imezio*, and others *Bigio antico*.

Greco brecciato scuro.—Mottled and clouded grey. *Vat. Inscriptions.*

Greco dislocato.—Bluish white, with parallel lines of grey, interrupted and turned out of their course as if by dislocation.

S. Giov. e Paolo; S. Sabina; S. Susanna; S. M. Domn.

Greco scritto (*tratteggiato*).—Yellowish or greenish white, suffused with grey, and scrawled with marks like letters.

S. Lor. in Borgo; S. Niccolò in Carcere; Albani.

G. s. confuso (letters indistinct). *S. Bernardino.*

Greco venato.—White, with parallel streaks of grey in various shades. Lines very fine and numerous; occasionally zigzag. *S. M. Cosm.—Albani.*

BIANCO E NERO ANTICO.

MARMOR PROCONNESIUM.—From the Island of Proconnesus, in the Sea of Marmora.

Dusty veined black, with angular stains of white; or white ground, with angular fragments of black.

S. Cecilia; Chiesa Nuova; S. Ignazio; S. M. Maggiore; S. Pietro; S. M. Via.—Barberini.

B. e N. dorato (gilded). *S. M. Maggiore.*

Bianco e Nero di Egitto.—Quarries unknown. It probably does not come from Egypt, but derives its name from imitations of Egyptian statues wrought in this marble. It is sometimes called *Occhio di Pavone nero*, because of its round white circlets.

Black, with marks of greyish white snails, in crescents or semi-circles.

S. Paolo alla Regola; S. Saba.—Egypt.

Bianco e Nero tigrato.—Misnamed by some writers a granite, and called by others *B. e N. granitoide*, from its granite-like markings.

Evenly distributed pools of black and white, with suspicion of pink and bluish grey.

S. Ant. Port.; S. Prassede; S. Rocco; S. M. Trast. Borghese; Torlonia.

BIANCO E NERO DI FRANCIA.

MARMOR CELTICUM.—Quarries unknown. Probably from the south of France.

Waves and streaks of impure black and white, with smears of yellowish brown.

S. Adriano; Chiesa Nuova; S. Cosma; S. Giov. Fior.; S. M. Vergini; S. M. Via.—B. N.

B. e Nero di Porto Ferrajo.—From the Island of Elba.

Impure black, untidily streaked with white.

S. Ambrogio; Ara Coeli; S. Lor. in Lucina.

B. e Nero di Perugia.—From quarries among the Umbrian hills.

Black, blotched and streaked with white, and mixed with untidy yellow. Black, plentifully scratched with white and pink.

S. Alessio; S. Dom.

NERO ANTICO.

MARMOR TAENARIUM.—From the promontory of Taenarum in Laconia.

Jet black, with faint streaks of pure white; or dusty black with greyish ribands.

S. Giov. Lat.; S. M. Angeli; S. M. Maggiore; S. Marcello; [*Regina Coeli*].

Borghese; Busts; Cap.; Doria.

N. bigiastro.—Ebony black, with bands of mottled white, brown and grey. *Cap.*

N. strisciato.—Black, with streaks of white.† *Consolazione.*

BIGIO ANTICO.

Marmor Batthium.—Probably from North Africa.
Light and dark grey in large patterns, with transparent surface and sparkling crystals.
S. Agost.; S. Catarina dei Funari; Consolazione; S. Lazzaro; S. Martino; S. Pietro; S. Salv. in Lauro; S. Urbano.—Albani.

B. alabastrino.—Suspicion of alabaster.
S. Anastasia.

B. azurrognolo.—Semi-transparent grey, with red or yellow veins. *S. Lor. in Borgo; S. Martino.*

B. bicolore.—Two shades of mottled grey. *Cand.*

B. brecciato.—Dark grey, with semi-transparent fragments of lighter hue.
S. Marco; S. Spirito; S. Pietro (Madonna).—*Camera.*

B. brecciato chiaro.—Light grey, with white oblong pebbles. *S. Cosma Trast.*

B. brecciato macchiato.—Black, with irregular small roundish pebbles of light grey, closely set together. *Sacristy.*

† Probably modern.

B. brecciato minuto.—Small markings of light and dark grey. *S. Lor. in Panis.; S. Sabina.*

B. brecciato minuto rossastro.—Light grey, with tiny pebbles in two shades, highly crystallised and tinged with pink. *S. Ant. Port.*

B. brecciato minuto schietto.—Uniform mottling of dark and light grey, in small patterns.
S. And. Quir.

B. chiaro.—Very light grey, with still lighter markings, and hair lines of brown.
S. Cecilia; S. Greg.; S. M. Grazie; S. Paolo.— Cand.; Terme.

B. chiaro dorato.—Yellowish streaks. *Cand.*

B. cipollino dorato.—Parallel lines of grey, streaked with gold. *Cand.*

B. conchigliare.—Clouded grey, with large slugs of lighter hue. *S. Angelo Pesc.*

B. cupo macchiato.—Dark grey, spotted with white. *S. Spirito in Sassia.*

B. dislocato.—Short interrupted lines of bluish grey on lighter ground. *Albani; Doria.*

B. dorato.—Wavy lines of grey, azure and yellow. *Cand.*

B. a fortezzino (*alabastrino*).—Large eyes of light

grey, divided by lines of wavy and angular grey, bordered with brown. *S. Apollinare.*

B. intrecciato.—Bluish grey, interlaced in shades. *S. Pancrazio.*

B. listato.—Narrow bands of dark grey and white. *S. Bart.; S. Giov. Fior.; S. Stef. Rotondo.*

B. lumacato grande.—Dark grey, with large white snails. *S. Girol.*

B. lum. chiaro.—Light grey, with lighter snails. *S. Vitale.—Cand.*

B. lumachellato.—Brownish or bluish grey, with white snails. *S. Greg.; S. Lor. Borgo; S. M. Cosm.; S. M. Orto; Sacristy; Trin. Pell.—Camera; Garden.*

B. lumachellato piccolo.—Light grey, with round or elliptical white snails. *S. Cecilia.*

B. macchiato nerastro.—Nearly jet black, with blotches of dirty white. *Chiaramonti.*

B. macchiato scuro.—Light brownish grey, veined and splashed with white, and spotted or scratched with brown. *S. Fr. Rom.; S. Pietro.*

B. ossifero chiaro.—Narrow oblong chips of grey on lighter ground. *Cand.*

B. perlato.—Pearly grey, with stains of white. *S. Dom.—Animali.*†

B. recticolato.—Finely netted. *Oct.*

* **B. rossastro lumachellato.**—Dark grey, handsomely blotched with pink, and full of broken shells. *Lat. Mus.*

B. scritto.—Light grey, scrawled with darker shade. *S. Cecilia; S. Clemente.—Albani.*

B. scritto reticolato.—Light grey, dashed crossways with chips of darker hue. *S. Stef. Rotondo.*

B. scuro macchiato.—Almost jet black, faintly marked with grey or clouded with white. *S. Bart.*

B. turchiniccio.—Bluish grey. *Cand.*

B. venato.—Light mottled grey, with veins of yellowish brown or black.
S. Pietro in Vincoli; Priorato; S. Pudenziana; Trin. Monti.—Albani; Cand.

B. venato di giallo.—Dark grey, stained with clouded white, and cross-streaked with forked white and gold. *S. Greg.*

B. venato scuro.—Smoky grey, with tortuous veins of dusky black. *Inscriptions.*

---

† Belli calls this beautiful marble *Bigio bardiglio*, and says that it comes from Carrara; but he is probably mistaken.

BIGIO MORATO.

MARMOR LUCULLEUM.—From the Island of Melos on the Nile.
Dusty powdered black, with faint streaks and spots of grey.
S. Giac. Corso; S. M. Grazie; S. Greg.; Sacristy. —Chiaramonti; Doria; Egypt; Mus. Torlonia.
B. morato ad Occhi.—Dark grey, with pools of lighter shade. *S. M. Scala.*

B. morato dorato.—Black, with veins of gold.
S. Pietro (Tommaso).
B. mor. lumachellato.—Black, with tiny white fragments of shells. *Cap.*
B. morato ondulato.—Greyish black, with round marks of light grey. *S. M. Traspontina.*

B. morato orbicolare.—Bluish black, with round stains of dusty black. *S. Niccolò Tol.*

B. morato venato.—Dark grey, with oblong stains of light grey and white veins. *Borgia.*

B. e Nero minuto.—Tiny shattered fragments of white, on light and dark grey.
S. And. Valle; S. Ant. Port.

BARDIGLIO.

Bardiglio antico.—From Carrara and Massa. Uniform slate colour; fine grain; no crystals.
Gesù e Maria; S. Martina; S. Nicc. Tolentino.

B. dorato.—Light grey, mottled with blue and dashed with gold. *Borgia.*

B. fiorito listato.—Striped grey, in many shades. *S. M. Maggiore.*

B. listellato.—Two shades of grey, in narrow parallel ribands. *S. Croce; S. Paolo fuori.*

B. venato chiaro.—Light bluish grey, with darker veins. *Muses.*

III. COLOURED MARBLES.

GIALLO ANTICO.

Marmor Numidicum.—Supposed to have been brought from Numidia, where no quarries however have been found. Large quantities of this marble, exhibiting many beautiful varieties, have been discovered on mountain flanks in Algeria.

Pale yellow, flushed with deeper yellow, and finely veined with purple.

Ara Coeli; Chiesa Nuova; S. Giov. Lat.; S. Luigi; S. Marco; S. M. Cosm.; S. Pietro Montorio; S. Pudenziana; S. Silv. Capite.—Arch of Drusus; Borghese.

G. alabastrino.—Patched with alabaster.
S. Fr. Rom.

G. bigiastro.—Veined with grey. *S. Greg.; S. M. Orto.*

G. brecciato.—Reddish brown clay, with yellow and white pebbles.
S. Catarina Fun.; S. Giov. Fior.; S. Giov. Lat.; Minerva; S. M. Popolo; Via; Pantheon; S. Pietro in Montorio.—Altemps; Animali; Cand.

G. brecciato bruno.—Brown pebbles, on whitish yellow. *S. M. Minerva.*

G. brecciato dorato.—Gilded pebbles in a paste of purplish red.
S. And. Valle; [S. Faustino]; S. Pietro.

G. brecciato pallido.—Yellowish brown, with pebbles of pale rosy white.
S. Dom. Sisto; S. M. Angeli; S. Seb.

G. brecciato pallido rossastro.—Pale yellow, with pinkish brown pebbles.
S. Pietro (Erasmus and Wenceslaus).

G. brecciato principe.—Pure violet ground, spotted with white; pebbles of bright creamy yellow.
S. Ignazio (shattered gold on purple): *S. M. Traspontina* (orange pebbles on red).

G. carnagione.—Flesh colour and pink, stained with dusty brownish yellow.
S. Agost.; S. Giov. Lat.; S. M. Vittoria: S. Seb. —Albani; Animali; Cand.; Terme.

G. carnagione disfatto.—Fleshy red, broken and crushed. *S. Crisogono.*

G. carnagione tigrato.—Stains of fleshy red, untidily surrounded by greyish white.
Pal. Madama; S. Pietro in Vincoli.

G. dorato.—Gilded yellow, with purplish veins.
Monti; S. Pietro; Arch of Constantine.

G. dorato cupo.—Dark gilded yellow.
Chiesa Nuova.

G. dorato piritifero.—Gold and rose, with black spots showing crystals of sulphate of iron.
S. M. Vittoria.

G. fasciato.—Yellow, banded with white.
[*S. Faustino.*]

G. focato.—Uniform pink, caused by the action of fire.
S. And. Valle; S. Cecilia; S. Silv. Quir.

G. melleo.—Honey-coloured yellow, with large stains of light grey and smaller ones of white.
S. Bernardino.

G. nuvolato.—White, plentifully clouded with light yellowish brown in parallel curves.
S. Giov. Lat.; S. Rocco; Trin. Pell.

G. paglino.—Uniform straw colour.
S. M. Vittoria.

Giallo pallido.—Cream coloured, streaked with rose or chocolate, and spotted with bluish grey.
S. Catarina Fun.; S. Giov. Lat.

G. picchiettato.—Pale and golden yellow, minutely unctured or lichened with brown.
S. M. di Loreto.
G. rossastro.—Pinkish yellow. *B. N.*
G. sfrangiato.—Yellow and light brown, disposed ı lumps like raw silk. *Sacristy.*
G. solforato.—Uniform bright sulphur colour.
S. Paolo alle Tre Fontane; S. Pietro (Colonna).
G. venato.—Yellow, veined with white.
S. M. Vittoria.

GIALLO TIGRATO.

M. CORINTHIUM.—From Corinth.
Indistinct and clouded mixture of pure white, pale ᵡhity brown, and lilac grey, plentifully flushed with ink. Ground of yellowish or pinkish grey lichen; reccia of rosy or yellowish grey pebblets, always ordered with grey or brown. Very pale yellow, louded with bluish grey.
S. Andrea della Valle; S. M. Maggiore.
G. tigrato pallido.—General hue paler. *Cand.*

GIALLO DI SIENA.

A handsome marble, quarried at Montarenti and ther places near Siena, but unknown to the ancients. t can never be mistaken for *Giallo antico;* but the echnical difference, where a small specimen only is btainable, consists in the entire absence of fine ortuous purple veins—an unfailing characteristic of he ancient marble, in all its varieties.

Giallo di Siena.—Dull yellow, netted with black.
Sacristy; Albani. •

G. di Siena brecciato.—Brown and white, with yellow stones.
S. Gius. Lungara.

G. di Siena dorato.—Uniform golden yellow, with no flush of pink, and no purple veins.
Oratorio di S. Giov.

G. di Siena venato.—Bright yellow, veined with black. *S. M. Vittoria.*

G. e Nero di Siena.—Bright yellow, plentifully netted with black. *S. Catarina da Siena.*

GIALLO E NERO ANTICO.

MARMOR RHODIUM.—From the Island of Rhodes. Black, veined with golden yellow.
* *S. Pietro ; S. Pudenziana.*

Giallo e Nero di Porto Venere.—Similar to the last, but distinguished by its triangular patches of dull yellow at the intersection of the veins.
S. Ambrogio; S. And. Valle; S. M. Popolo; Trin. Pell.; S. Vitale.—Cap.

Porto Venere schizzato (scratched).—*Terme.*
P. V. venato (with white veins).—*S. P. Montorio.*

ROSSO ANTICO.

Marmor Taenarium.—From the Promontory of Taenarum in Laconia, now Cape Matapan.

Dark red, with parallel hair lines of darker hue; broad yellowish streaks; texture of raw beef; patches of fleecy white and bluish grey.

S. Bibiana; S. Pietro Vincoli; S. Prassede.

Animali; Borghese; Busts; Cand.; Cap.; Colonna; Doria; Ludovisi; Masks; Octagon.

Rosso lumachellato.—Bright red, with evenly distributed flame-shaped spots of white.

* S. Cecilia.

Rosso porfidino.—Blood red, with tiny black points and no veins. *Masks.*

Rosso striato.—Dark red, with tiny veins of black and a zone of livid white.

S. M. Maggiore.—Rospigliosi; Cand.; Colonna.

IV. VEINED OR VARIEGATED MARBLES.

CIPOLLINO.

Marmor Carystium.—From Carystus in the Island of Euboea (Negroponte). These quarries have been long since exhausted, but some fine beds of a similar marble are now worked near Saillon in the Rhone Valley, about 6200 feet above the sea. Specimens may be seen at a shop in Queen Victoria Street, E.C.

Cipollino verde.—Apple green, with parallel wavy or zigzag lines of darker shade.
S. Greg.; S. Lor. fuori; S. Luigi; S. Martino; S. Pietro; S. Salv. Lauro.—Colonna; Doria.

C. verde chiaro.—Green brighter and more abundant.
Divino Amore; S. Rocco; Sacristy; Via Lata.— Camera.

C. verde giallastro.—Greyish green, waved with dark green, brown, and yellow.
Minerva; Piazza di Spagna.

C. verde increspato.—Narrow zones of white and green, interlacing and confused.
S. Nicc. Carcere.—Cand.; Inscriptions.

C. verde zonale.—Bands very clearly defined.
S. Lor. Miranda; S. Nicc. Carcere.

C. verde prasio.—Pale whitish green, with very bright streaks of emerald.
S. Nicc. Carcere; Borghese; Mus. Torlonia.

C. verde ondato.—Dirty pinkish white, with confused bands of light and dark green.
* *S. Gius. Lungara; S. Pietro; S. Teodoro.*

C. verde rigato.—Lines more distinctly ruled.
S. Paolo Tre Font.—Albani.

C. marino.—Closely set, and tortuous lines of dark grey and white, on greenish lilac ground.
S. Carlo al Corso; Gesù; Minerva.

C. marino minuto.—Veins finer. *Cand.*

C. marino violetto.—Greenish lilac, veined with violet and patched with pinky white. *Albani.*

C. ondato.—Greenish white, tortuously veined with greenish grey. *S. Gioacchino.—Cap.*

C. bigio.—Dark snail grey, with closely set parallel streaks of every shade.
Angeli Custodi; Sacristy; S. Stef. Cacco; S. Vitale.

C. bigio rigato.—Knotted lines of yellowish white and grey. *S. Cecilia.—B. N.*

C. bigio e nero.—Bands of ashy grey and black. *B. N.*

C. bigiastro.—Light grey, with greyish lines. *Etruscan Mus.*

C. nero.—Jet black bands; wavy lines of grey and greenish grey. *S. Pietro; Sacristy.*

Cipollino rosso.—Parallel lines of dark purple, red, rose, and pink, knotted like timber. Broad striated veins of fleshy white, resembling beef fat.
Ara Coeli; S. Cesareo; S. Giov. Paolo; S. Greg.; S. Marco; S. M. Popolo; S. Paolo; S. Pietro Vincoli; S. Salv. Lauro.

C. rosso brecciato.—Dull red, with large pebbles. *Lat. Mus.*

C. rosso diasprato.—Dark red, black, and a little white, disposed like jasper. *Chiesa Nuova.*

C. rosso fasciato.—Light red, banded with dark red and livid white. *S. Giov. Lat.*

C. rosso macchiato.—Red, lightly veined and spotted with white. *Biga ; Croce Greca.*

C. pavonazzo scuro.—Dark purple, with waves of light purple and red. *Scala Santa.*

C. mandolato verde.—Much of this is modern, from quarries in the Pyrenees and at Caunes. The French call it *Campan Vert*, and there is a good deal of it in the *Conservatoire des Arts et Métiers*, at Paris.

Longitudinal almond-shaped pebbles, bordered with fine streaks of green or blue, on yellowish green ground. *Gesù ; S. Giov. Paolo ; S. Pietro Vincoli ; S. Stef. Cacco ; S. Vitale.*

C. mandolato verde grande.—Larger markings. *S. Giov. Lat.*

C. m. verde giallastro.—Yellowish. *Cosmedin.*

C. m. verde minuto.—Tiny white pebbles on light green, bordered with black lines. *Ara Coeli.*

C. m. lionato.—Tawny red, with darker veins and lighter spots. *Trin. Pell.—Mus. Arch.*

C. m. lionato chiaro.—Mottled pink, brown, and white. * *Consolazione.*

C. m. rosso.—Small almond-shaped mottling of dusky red and bluish grey (modern).
S. Lucia in Selci; S. M. Popolo.
C. pavonazzo.—Narrow bands of purple.
* *Consolazione.*

COTTANELLO.

Named after the district in which it is found, near Moricone, about forty miles from Rome, among the Sabine hills. The quarries were worked by the Romans, who appear to have found a superior quality of marble, the supply of which is now exhausted. The modern species, as employed at S. Pietro and elsewhere, is very coarse and unattractive. There are good columns of the ancient kind in the Cathedral, and Church of S. Filippo, at Spoleto.

C. antico.—Very pale bricky red, veined with pure white. *Gesù.—Cap.*

C. antico pav.—Purple brown, with very fine close grain. *Mus. Arch.*

C. dorato.—Greenish yellow and violet, minutely streaked with brown and dashed with white. Entire absence of brick red. *S. Giov. Fior.*

C. giallo.—Whitish yellow and pale red, with numerous white veins and flame-shaped blotches. *S. Pietro; SS. Pietro e Marcellino.*

C. rosso scuro.—Uniform reddish brown, with small streaks of pure white. *S. And. Quir.*

FIORE DI PERSICO.

MARMOR MOLOSSIUM.—From Epirus. Perhaps some of the varieties come from Elba. In form and disposition of markings, though not in colour, it sometimes bears a strong resemblance to *Cottanello*.
Lilac, peach blossom, red, and white, in flowery patterns.

S. Ant. Port.; S. Giov. Paolo; S. Martino; S. M. Itria; [Regina Coeli]; Scala Coeli; Vittoria.—Conservatori.

F. di Persico brecciato.—Lilac and white pebbles on red. *Suffragio.*

F. di Persico bruniccio.—Purple and white, in form of flames, with stains of brown and red. *Minerva.*

F. di Persico chiaro.—Very light lavender.
S. Eligio; S. Susanna.

F. di Persico confuso.—Curiously mottled light grey, white, and chocolate. *S. Carlo Catinari.*

F. di Persico giallastro.—Lilac and lavender, with yellowish hue. *S. Carlo Catinari.*

F. di Persico macchiato.—Light lavender, with foliated veins of darker hue, purple spots, and tinge of pinkish yellow.
S. M. Campitelli; S. Pietro Vinc.

F. di Persico minuto.—Markings very small.
S. Pietro (S. Processo).

F. di Persico pavonazzo.—Flushed lilac, veined with purple and streaked with fleecy white.
S. Prassede.
F. di Persico picchiettato.—Veined lilac, pricked with purple and spotted with yellowish white.
S. Croce dei Lucchesi.
F. di Persico reticolare.—Lilac in several shades, with crossed lines like network.
Chiesa Nuova; Gesù; S. Pudenziana.—Albani; Borgia.
F. di Persico rossigno.—Pinkish brick red and greyish white, with veins of light transparent blue.
Ara Coeli.
F. di Persico rosso.—Red, white, and lilac, streaked with yellow.
S. Eustachio; S. M. Traspontina; S. Silv. Quir.; Rospigliosi.
F. di Persico sanguigno.—Blood-red stains.
S. Giov. Fior.
F. di Persico venato.—Lilac, veined with purple.
S. Giuseppe Lungara.—Terme.
F. di Persico violetto.—Shades of violet.
S. Seb.

PAVONAZZETTO.

MARMOR SYNNADICUM.—From quarries near Synnada in Phrygia.

Very dark brownish purple ground, with hue of clotted blood and slightly metallic texture. Large pebbles of

semi-transparent creamy white, tinged with orange, pink, or green.
S. Anastasia; Ara Coeli; S. Giov. Lat.; S. Lor. fuori; S. M. Cosm.; S. Martino; S. Sabina.—Barberini; Lat. Mus.

Pav. argentino.—Silvery.
S. Vitale; Mus. Torlonia.

Pav. azzurrigno.—Light blue, with fragments of yellowish and greenish white.
Minerva; S. Salv. Lauro.

* **Pav. argentino reticolato.**—Fine network of silvered purple. S. Tommaso in Formis.

Pav. bianco.—Nearly all white.
Chiesa Nuova; ·SS. Nereo Ach.; Animali.

Pav. bianco venato.—Pinkish white, with reticulated veins. S. Giov. Paolo; S. Onofrio.

Pav. bigio brecciato.—White pebbles, on finely mottled greyish purple. Consolazione; Suffragio.

Pav. bigio brecciato argentino.—Greyish pebbles, with flush of silver. Albani.

Pav. bigio verdognolo brecciato.—Greyish pebbles, with tinge of green. Animali.

Pav. bigiastro reticolato.—Network of purple and silvery grey on white. S. M. Grazie.

Pav. brecciato.—Purple, with fragments of white.
S. Agnese fuori; S. M. Via; S. Pietro; S P.

Montorio; S. Silv. Quir.; S. Spirito; S. Stef. Cacco; Vittoria.—Borghese; Siciliana.

Pav. brecciato argentino.—Silvery hue. *S. Marco; Via Lata; Cand.*

Pav. br. dorato.—Dark chocolate, with flushed and crystallised white pebbles. *S. Fr. Ripa; S. M. Scala; Sacristy; S. P. Vincoli. Ludovisi.*

Pav. br. fiorito.—Metallic golden green, with pebbles of pinkish cream and grey. *Altemps.*

Pav. br. minuto.—Reddish purple, crammed with minute fragments of livid white. *S. Clemente.—Animali.*

Pav. cenerognolo.—Ashy green, pure purple, and white. *S. Luigi.*

Pav. cupo.—Very dark purple with yellowish white pebbles. *S. Greg.*

Pav. cupo reticolato.—Beautifully netted. *Conservatori.*

Pav. dorato.—Purple, flushed with gold. *B. Rita.*

Pav. ad inchiostro.—Dark purple, with inky streaks. *Belvedere.*

Pav. nero.—Purple, almost black. *S. Croce.*

Pav. policromo.—Handsome blending of purple and lilac in many shades. *S. Paolo.*

Pav. sanguigno.—Beef red, with fragments of reddish white. *Minerva.*

Pav. sanguigno confuso.—Similar, but lines less distinct. *S. Pudenziana.*

Pav. scuro angoloso.—Brown, with yellowish white pebbles. *S. Agnese fuori; S. N. Prefetti.*

Pav. tigrato.—Uniformly distributed pools of lilac and white.
S. Lor. fuori; S. M. Angeli; Pantheon; S. Paolo.

Pav. turchiniccio.—Small oblong white fragments on bluish ground. *S. Pietro* (Colonna).

Pav. venato.—Creamy white, netted and veined with purple. *SS. Nereo Ach.*

Pav. verde.—Here and there a vein of bright green. *S. Bart.; Albani.*

Pav. verdiccio.—Greenish purple, with pebbles of livid white and yellow. *Chiesa Nuova. Chiaramonti.*

BIANCO E GIALLO ANTICO.

M. PHENGITE.—From Cappadocia.

White, with veins of light yellow, over which are hair lines of a darker shade. Corsi says that this marble received so bright a polish (φέγγειν, to glisten) as to reflect objects like a mirror; and that for this reason Domitian had a corridor lined with it, in the hope of protecting himself against assassination as he walked along. I have never succeeded in finding a specimen of it, and Corsi himself appears to have discovered only one tiny slab, which he picked up at the mouth of a drain near the Tiber, and placed in his collection. It must either have been destroyed wholesale as quicklime in the middle ages, or else the marble must be a myth, some highly translucent alabaster having probably been mistaken for it. By way of conjecture, I offer as a possible example a slab in *SS. Giov. e Paolo*.

PORTA SANTA.

M. JASSENSE.—From the Island of Jasus, off the coast of Caria in the Archipelago. Mr. Brindley found quarries of it in the Island of Chios. A similar marble, vastly inferior in beauty, colour, and consistency, is common near Siena and in several parts of northern Italy. The name is derived from the 'Sacred Gate' of the four great Basilicas—S. Pietro, S. Giov. in Laterano, S. M. Maggiore, and S. Paolo—the doorjambs of which are made of this marble. They are opened by the Pope himself only in jubilee years—the 25th, 50th, 75th, and 100th of each century.

The colours and markings of this marble are so infinite that I have thought it best to place all the columns and large masses under a general heading, and to describe the smaller examples of rare or specially attractive varieties as they occur on altars or *cancelli*. The surface of the fountain-basins in the *Piazza Colonna* and *P. Navona*, if sawn up into slabs for specimens, would furnish almost all the varieties in Rome.

Pink, lilac, or flesh colour, in irregular mottlings or patches, with tortuous veins of white and red. Almost every hue is sometimes visible, except green.

S. Agost.; S. Anastasia; S. And. Fratte; Ara Coeli; S. Carlo Cat.; S. Cecilia; Chiesa. Nuova; S. Fr. Ripa; Gesù; S. Giov. Fior.; S. Greg.; S. Marcello; S. Marco; S. M. Maggiore; S. M. Via; Minerva; S. Pancrazio; Traspontina; Trin. Pell. Cap.; Papa Giulio; Piazza Colonna; P. Navona; Rospigliosi; Terme; Via del Cardello.

* **P. S. alabastrina.**—Colours bright and variegated, with streaks resembling alabaster.

S. Salv. Onda; Busts.

P. S. arlecchina.—Patched lilac and grey.

S. M. Maggiore; Vittoria.

P. S. bicolore.—Patches of flesh colour and grey.

S. Croce; S. Pietro (Michele).

P. S. bigia.—Dull grey, veined with white and red.

S. M. Monti; S. N. Carcere; S. Pietro (Present.).

P. S. bigia brecciata.—Grey pebbles. *Terme.*

P. S. bigia dorata.—Bluish grey, with gloss of gold. *Sacristy.*

P. S. bigia fiorita.—Very dark uniform grey, finely curled and streaked with red and reddish brown.

S. Carlo Cat.

P. S. bigia nuvolata.—Clouded and mottled grey, streaked with white and red. *S. Salv. Lauro.*

P. S. bigia orbicolare.—Light grey, crammed with round stains of grey and flesh colour.
Chiesa Nuova; S. Giov. Lat.; S. Spirito.

P. S. brecciata.—Mottled pink, with irregular patches of dark grey, small angular flesh-coloured pebbles, and streaks of pure white.
S. M. Scala; S. Girolamo della Carità; S. Mich. Ripa.

P. S. brecciata lumacata.—Yellowish grey pebbles on brownish red, with streaks of white and a few white snails. *S. Agata Trast.*

P. S. brecciata minuta.—Small flesh-coloured pebbles on dark reddish brown.
S. Balbina; S. Marco.—Terme.

P. S. bruna bicolore.—Patches of bluish grey and reddish brown. *S. Eustachio.*

P. S. bruna giallastra.—Yellowish brown. *Minerva.*

P. S. bruna e rossastra.—Brown and pink. *Agonizzanti.*

P. S. carnagione.—Flesh colour. *S. Anastasia.*

P. S. carnina.—Flesh colour, finely veined and curled with red and lilac. *Minerva.*

P. S. cerulea.—Sky blue. *S. M. Itria ; Scala Coeli.*

P. S. fasciata.—Banded. *S. M. Maggiore.*

P. S. florita.—Reddish grey and flesh colour upon yellowish red, veined with white.
S. Agnese fuori ; S. And. Valle ; Minerva.
P. S. gialla cerulea.—Flints of light bluish grey embedded in dull brown, with streaks of pure white.
S. M. Pace.
P. S. gialla rossastra.—Pink and yellow.
Chiesa Nuova.
P. S. giallastra brecciata.—Yellowish red, with fragments of pink, and livid white.
S. M. Monserrato.
P. S. lionata.—Tawny, with grey fragments bordered white. *S. Giov. Fior.*

P. S. lionata ramificata.—Tawny, with branching veins. *S. Agnese fuori.*

P. S. lumacata.—Here and there a small white or pink shell.
[*S. Faustino*]; *S. Salv. Lauro.—Albani.*
P. S. madreporitica.—Purplish red, with round white or yellowish fragments of madrepore.
S. Pietro (Choir).—*B. N.*
P. S. pallida.—Very pale. *S. Giov. Lat.*

P. S. pavonazza intrecciata.—Network of purple, red, and blue. *S. Onofrio.*

P. S. ranciata.—Orange, with fragments of fleshy red, foliated in black. *Sala Regia.*

P. S. reticolata.—Faded red, covered with network of brighter hue. *S. Luigi.*

P. S. rossa.—Light red, livid white, azure, and blue. *S. Pietro* (Present.); *S. Spirito.*

P. S. rossa brecciata.—Pinkish brick, with pebbles of white, flesh colour, and grey.
S. N. Carcere ; S. Silv. Quir. ; Vittoria.

P. S. rossa reticolata.—Shades of pink, plentifully veined with curly lines of dark red. *Vittoria.*

P. S. rossastra.—Pink, with bluish pebbles.
S. Giac. in Borgo ; Minerva.

P. S. rossastra brecciata scura.—Reddish chocolate, with bluish grey pebbles and dashes of pure white.
S. Catarina ; S. Giov. Lat. ; S. Giov. Pigna.

P. S. rossastra conchigliare.—Raw beef, with very finely engrained streaks of white.
Chiesa Nuova ; S. Pantaleo.

P. S. tigrata.—Metallic yellowish green and fleecy white, flushed with pink.
S. Agost. ; S. Luigi.

P. S. venata.—Veined with white.
S. Pietro (S. Michele); *Trin. Monti.*
P. S. venata a Stuoia.—Rosy lilac, with parallel lines of purple at regular intervals, and cross lines of the same colour. Faint streaks of white.
S. Sabina; Vittoria; *Octagon.*
P. S. violacea.—Violet red, with white veins.
**S. Ambrogio; Cap.*
P. S. violacea poligonia.—Violet red and black, with no visible cement, like a Cyclopean wall.
S. And. Valle; S. Dorotea.

ROSSO DI FRANCIA.

From *Caunes*, in the S.E. of France.
Red, with large stains, like pebbles of flinty blue, very irregular in outline. Modern, and unattractive.
S. Anastasia; S. M. Anima; S. Pietro.

TAORMINA BRECCIATO.

Very like the last, and possibly identical with it; but the colours are more distinct, and the markings rather handsome. Corsi calls it a Sicilian jasper, with which marble it appears to have nothing whatever in common. Greyish violet and red.
S. Ambrogio; S. Dionigi; S. Gir. Carità; S. Giov. Lat.; S. Marco; S. Rocco; S. Silv. Quir.; Scuola Castigliana.

V. SHELL MARBLES.

LUMACHELLA.

Except in the cases where the prevenance is stated, as in *Lum. di Egitto*, it is not known from whence these marbles came. Most of them are ancient, but the first-named species is entirely modern, and is quarried not far from Aquila.

Lumachella degli Abruzzi. — Light buff grey, crowded with tiny shells of the same hue, and larger ones of slate blue.

S. M. Maggiore; S. Pudenziana; Trin. Monti.

Lum. bigia.—Light brown, densely crowded with very minute fragments of black and transparent greyish white.

S. And. Valle; Ara Coeli; Minerva.

Lum. bigia.—Grey, veined with brown and full of broken white shells. *S. Lor. fuori.*

Lum. bigia bruna.—Black, peppered with grey and crowded with large white snails. Faint flush of rose. *Chiesa Nuova.*

Lum. bigia giallastra.—Grey, tinged with yellow. *S. Salv. Lauro; Borghese.*

Lum. bigia orientale.—Bluish grey, with numerous white snails. * *S. M. Via Lata.*

Lum. bigia rossastra.—Grey, flushed with pink. *S. M. Popolo.*

Lum. bigia di Egitto.—Densely crowded grey snails, with a few yellowish white. Flush of pinkish brown. *Angeli Custodi; Minerva; Vittoria; S. Onofrio.—Cap.*

Grey, with white and blue snails and a little gold. B. *S. M. Aquiro.*

Bluish grey, with yellowish white snails. *Cap.; Terme.*

Lum. bruna rossastra.—Brownish grey, flushed with pink. *Borghese.*

* **Lum. di Calabria.**—Peppered brownish grey, with bluish snails, and fragments of white spiral shells. *SS. Simone Giuda.*

Lum. gialla di Egitto.—Golden yellow, with snails of bright yellow and bluish grey. *S. M. Traspontina; S. Onofrio.*

Lum. gialla.—Large yellow snails with grey chips. *Chiesa Nuova.*

Lum. gialla bigiastra min.—Close-grained light brown, with grey and yellowish snails. *Conservatori.*

* **Lum. gialla e pavonazza.**—Dark brown, with orange shells and snails. Chocolate, densely crowded with minute yellow chips, and circlets having brown centres. *Gesù; S. M. Scala; Minerva.*

Lum. lionata.—Reddish brown, blotched with pink. Suspicion of white and yellow. *S. And. Valle.*

Lum. nera.—Bronze, with tiny streaks of yellowish brown.

S. Onofrio; Gesù; S. Lor. fuori; S. M. Pace; Trin. Pell.

Lum. nera minuta.—Jet black, with numerous small curly white snails. * *S. Agost.; S. Lor. Lucina.*

Lum. pavonazza.—Purple, peppered with tiny white fragments. A few rosy flints.

S. Bernardo; S. Dorotea.

Lum. pav. disfatta.—Very much broken.

S. M. Consolazione.

Lum. persichina.—Lilac. *Inscriptions.*

Lum. rosea.—Pale chalky rose and yellow, crowded with small narrow slugs. *Gesù Maria; Sciarra.*

Lum. rossa.—Uniform crimson and semi-transparent white.

S. Carlo Cat.; S. Onofrio; S. Rocco.

Red, with greyish white madrepores.

S. Giov. Fior.

Lum. rossa minuta.—Red, with tiny fragments. *Cand.*

Lum. violetta.—Violet, tinged with blood red. Snails white or grey, touched with gold.

S. And. Valle.

Lumachellone antico.—Earthy grey, with large snails. * *S. Paolo fuori.*

Lumachellone bigio.—Large grey snails and small white shells. * *S. Pancrazio.*

ASTRACANE.

Said to come from Agra, though it was formerly believed to have been brought from Astrakhan, near the shores of the Caspian Sea.

Astracane giallo R.—Brownish orange, with fine fragments of slate-coloured snails, tinged with pink (*verdastro maschio* B). *S. And. Valle ; S. M. Via.*

Brownish yellow, finely peppered with black and faintly marked with white. R.

S. M. Scala ; Minerva ; S. Stef. Cacco.

A. bruno.—Dull blackish grey, on raw brick ground. R.

S. And. Valle ; Chiesa Nuova ; Trin. Pell.

Astracane femina.—Dull yellowish brown, with transparent snails like gum, and stains of violet.

S. Gir. Carità ; S. Lor. Fonte.

Astracane rossastro.—Similar, with pinkish hue. *Lat. Mus. ; Mus. Torlonia.*

BROCCATELLO.

MARMOR SCHISTON.—From Tortosa in Spain, where it is still quarried. This handsome marble is extensively used as a surface ornament in the Roman churches, but has never been a favourite for columns.

Broccatello giallo. — Pale yellow, rivered with brown and embedded with crystal snails of purplish yellow.

S. Calisto; S. Cecilia; S. M. Pace; S. Paolo; S. Stef. Cacco.

Br. melleo. — Honey-coloured snails on purplish ground. *S. And. Valle; S. Cat. Funari.*

Br. pavonazzo cupo.—Finely mottled reddish purple; fragments of grey and golden shells tinged with pink.
S. M. Maggiore; Spirito Santo.

* **Br. principe.**—Mottled violet and yellow, with transparent chips of bluish white. Yellow snails with whitish centre. *Apostoli; S. M. Maggiore.*

Br. rosso.—Bright reddish brown, with lighter markings. *S. M. Pace.*

Br. sanguigno.—Washed-out blood red, with livid white snails. *SS. Cosma Damiano.*

OCCHIO DI PAVONE.

Occhio di Pavone pavonazzo.—Brick red, peppered with pearly white fragments. Oysters transparent, crystallised, and yellowish, with white circles. Suspicion of violet brown.

S. Gius. Lungara; Minerva; S. N. Tolentino; Quattro Coron.—Sapienza; Quirinal.

Occhio di Pav. pav. scuro.—Purple, with numerous shattered fragments of white. *Library.*

Occhio di Pav. pav. piccolo.—Markings very tiny. *Albani.*

Occhio di Pav. rosso B.—Red, with round or oval shells changing into white lime.
S. Alessio; S. M. Trast.; S. M. Via Lata; S. Pietro (Sapphira).—*Albani.*
Two shades of bricky red with chips and streaks of white and spots of pink. *Quirinal.*

Occhio di Pav. bruno.—Brownish red.
S. Gius. Lungara.
Occhio di Pav. verdognolo.—Tinge of green.
S. Bernardino B.

VI. BRECCIA.

The ancient quarries of all these marbles are unknown, and the formation is so general that some of them may perhaps have been brought from France or Northern Italy. A large number, however, undoubtedly came from Africa or the East, and many were probably imported from the neighbourhood of Hierapolis, and from the Greek Islands. To avoid splitting up into varieties, I have raised four species to the rank of *genera.*

Br. di Aleppo.—This marble is so very rare that there is no reason for doubting that it was brought from Aleppo. A very inferior kind with dull colours has been found near Serravezza, and a still coarser quality at Alet in France.

Slate grey, and gold pebbles on dull red.
S. Agost.; S. Lor. Fonte; S. M. Grazie; S. Onofrio; S. P. Vincoli; S. Pudenziana; Vittoria.—Borghese.

Br. di Aleppo principe.—Blood red, clouded with white pebbles, blotches of bright yellow, and a few violet snails. ** Cand.*

Br. di Aleppo rossa.—Dark reddish brown, with pebbles of very light pink and grey, and tinges of bright red. *Ara Coeli.*

Br. bianca e nera.—Untidy shattered mixture of black and white or muddy grey.
S. Anastasia; S. M. Maggiore.—Masks.

Br. bruna.—Large reddish brown pebbles inclining to violet. Suspicion of white. *Chiesa Nuova.*

* Br. della Villa Casali.—Lilac, grey, and gold pebbles on ground of shattered pink. *Museo Arch.*

Br. dorata.—Purple ground, tinged with white. Bright yellow pebbles.
Ara Coeli; S. Eusebio; S. Lucia Gonfalone; S. Marcello; S. M. Popolo; S. Paolo; S. P. Vincoli.

A few purple pebbles on yellow. *Minerva.*

Br. dorata minuta.—Tiny gold pebbles on lilac ground. *S. Costanza;* * *S. Susanna.*

Br. dor. oleosa. —Tiny violet pebbles set in purplish red, and tinged with green and gold. *S. Luigi.*

Br. dor. orbicolare.—Gold on violet, with round pebbles. *S. And. Valle.*

Br. dor. pavonazza.—Gold pebbles among purple, lilac, and bluish grey. *Altemps.*

Br. frutticolosa.—Round pebbles of yellowish grey and brown on drab ground. *S. Lor. Panis.*

Br. frutticolosa minuta.†—Small oval pebbles, with tiny truffles.
S. Agost.; S. Ambrogio; Conservatori.

Br. gialla.—Yellow pebbles on reddish purple, fleeced with white. *Minerva; Trast.*

Br. gialla fibrosa.—Tiny gilded cream pebbles on ground of rich gold. *Cap.*

Br. gialla rossastra.—Reddish violet, covered with chips and pebbles of cream colour and brownish grey. *S. Croce; S. Giov. Lat.; S. Greg.; S. M. Trast.*

† A gateway, theatre, and other Roman remains at Aosta are built entirely of this marble. It probably comes from the neighbourhood of Susa.

Br. gialla e pavonazza.—Yellow pebbles on violet ground. *Cap.*

Br. gialla e nera.—Very dark slate and faint clouded yellow.
S. Carlo Cat.; Cappuccini; S. Pudenziana.

Br. Gregoriana.—White, flushed with bright rose. *Ara Coeli; Chiesa Nuova; S. N. Arcioni.*

[**Br. lionata.**— R. Brownish red, clouded with darker hue. *Verona.*]

Br. marrone.—Dark bricky red, with small lighter pebbles in many shades.
S. And. Valle; Umiltà.

Br. minuta angolosa.—Tiny light brown angular pebbles on reddish brown. *S. M. Pace.*

Br. pavonazza.—Large pebbles of white and lilac, evenly distributed. Purple on light brown and white.
S. Eusebio; Gesù Maria; S. M. Monterone; B. Rita.—*Borgia; Sala Regia.*
Lilac and pure white long narrow pebbles on very dark violet ground. A good deal of light green. *Ara Coeli.*—*Castigliana.*

Pinkish white pebbles on broken ground of dark greyish purple. *Minerva.*

Gilded handsome grey on very dark ground.
S. P. Vincoli.

Br. pav. bianca.—Nearly all white, with dark purple veins. *S. Seb.*

Br. pav. bigiastra.—Greyish.
S. M. Liberatrice.

Br. pav. cioccolata.—Chocolate, with small lilac pebbles, and dashes of coarse white (*bruna* B).
Suffragio.

Br. pav. confuso.—Medley of white, red, and purple.
S. Adriano.

Br. pav. grande.—Large white oval pebbles on purple ground, very regular on distribution.
S. Ignazio; S. Pietro (Tribune).

Br. pav. lineare.—Very long greyish white stones on light lilac and violet ground. *S. Giac. Corso.*

Br. pav. livida.—Bluish white pebbles. *S. Paolo.*

Br. pav. minuta.—Flushed white on pink, and purple. Pebbles very small.
Ara Coeli; Chiesa Nuova; S. Giov. Genov.; Mus. Arch.

Br. pav. reticolata.—Netted. Pinkish white pebbles on purple.—*Inscriptions.*
S. Bernardo (mottled violet and grey); *S. Dom.*

Sisto (grey pebbles on chocolate); *S. Susanna* (cream pebbles on broken ground of violet).

Br. pav. rossastra.—Galantina of violet, pink, purple, and white, with delicate veining. *Albani.*

Br. pav. sfrangiata.—Shattered yellowish white on light purple.
S. Catarina Fun.; S. M. Angeli; S. Pietro (Erasmus).

Br. pav. venata.—White pebbles veined with purple. *Crypt.*

Br. pav. traccagnina B.—Brown, white, and pink.
S. Catarina; S. Clemente.

Br. pav. trac. minuta B.—Similar, but tiny.
S. Pietro (SS. Simon and Jude).

Br. pav. verdiccia.—Greenish hue. Brownish white pebbles on dark grey.
S. M. Traspontina.

Br. Quintilina.—Tortoise-shell pebbles, with a few golden, green, and almost black, on shattered ground of greyish lilac. *S. Catarina.*

Br. Quintilina dorata.—Pinkish white, with a few minute pebbles of brown, and larger ones of brownish red, all tinged with gold.
S. And. Valle; S. Dom.; S. Pudenziana.

Br. Qu. biancastra.—Flawed with white.
S. M. Maggiore; Vittoria.

Breccia rossa.—Ground violet, rarely pink; pebbles pink, violet, or reddish brown. *S. Carlo Cat.; S. M. Domnica; Monserrato; S. Pietro* (S. Michele); *S. Prisca; S. Salv. Lauro; S. Seb. Pallara; S. Spirito; S. Tommaso Cenci: Vittoria.—Camera.*

Br. rossa lumachellata.—Pink, red, and purple, with a few white snails. *S. Luigi.*

B. rossa minuta.—Pebbles smaller. *S. Salv. Lauro.*

B. rossa poligonia.—Large red and violet stones with parallel veins. *Vittoria.*

B. rossa e gialla.—Chocolate ground, powdered with white and crowded with angular bits of yellowish white. R. *S. Pietro.*

Br. rossa e gialla min.—Tiny pebbles of yellowish brown and pinkish white on lilac ground flushed with rose. S.
S. Lor. Panis.; S. M. Maggiore; Minerva.

Br. rossa e gialla frantumata (smashed into fragments). *S. M. Monti.*

Br. rossastra.—Pink. *S. Greg.*

B. rossa scura.—Colours less vivid. *S. M. Aquiro.*

Br. di S. Ipolito.—Modern. From quarries near Spoleto. The Church of S. Filippo in that city has four large columns veneered with it, and a handsome font of the same marble. Tiny pebblets of pink, brown, and yellow, evenly mixed, and about the size of peas.

S. *Onofrio;* SS. *Vincenzo Anast.—Borghese; Terme.*

Br. di S. Ipolito grande. — Similar, with rather larger pebbles of white and rose on pink.

S. *Luigi.*

Br. di Serravezza.—Yellowish white, inclining to pink, with purplish veins. Pebbles small, oblong or oval, and closely set.

S. *Lucia Gonfalone;* S. *M. Liberatrice;* S. *Prassede;* S. *Pudenziana.—Doria; Mus. Torlonia.*

Br. di Ser. pallida.—Colours less vivid.

S. *Ambrogio.*

Br. di Ser. pavonazza.—White pebbles on lilac ground.

S. *M. Vittoria;* S. *Martina;* S. *Seb.;* *Suffragio.* *—Borghese; Piazza di Spagna.*

Br. di Ser. persichina.—Violet pebbles mixed with white ones, on lilac ground. S. *N. Tolentino.*

Br. di Ser. macchiata.—Stained with less vivid colours. *Doria.*

Br. di Ser. fiorita.—Large and handsome blotches of lilac, purple, and yellowish white. *Gesù.*

Br. di Ser. mandolata.—Markings almond-shaped.

S. *M. Angeli.*

Br. di Ser. nobile.—Bright purple, with creamy pebbles and streaks of green. S. *Clemente.*

Br. di Simone—(Rossa Apennina).—Brick red, with pink pebbles and small white spots. Light brown on reddish brown.
Ara Coeli ; Chiesa Nuova ; S. M. Scala ; S. Pietro (Greg.) ; S. P. Vincoli.—Mus. Arch.

Br. di Simone diasprato.—Dark mottled brown and red, veined with white, and resembling jasper.
S. Giov. Paolo.

* **Br. di Svezia.**—Brick red, with small white and pink spots. *Albani.*

Br. verde.—Dark green pebbles on crushed light green with a few white pebbles.
S. Giac. Corso ; S. M. in Via.

Br. verde di Egitto.—Mr. Brindley found some quarries of this marble between Kossier and Koft, near Hamamat, in Egypt. Fragments of porphyry, granite, and various marbles, on ground of shattered greyish green.
Gesù ; S. And. delle Fratte ; S. Paolo.—Cand. ; Cap. ; Albani ; Mus. Torlonia.

Br. verde di Egitto minuta.—Similar, with smaller markings. *S. Pietro Vincoli.*

Br. verde di Egitto porfiroide.—Light green, with pebbles of dark green, pink, white, and greenish yellow. Dark longitudinal porphyry chips. *Conservatori.*

Br. verde di Egitto scura.—Green, powdered with

gold and silver. Pebbles black, green, and pinkish grey. *Apostoli; V. Albani.*

Br. verde di Genova.—Metallic, and plentifully flawed with pure white. *Cand.*

BRECCIA CORALLINA.

This marble is named after its cement, which is usually of coral colour, though there is often very little of it, and sometimes none at all. The pebbles are most frequently red, pink, white, or yellow.

Corallina antica.—Bright coral red and pinkish white.
Ara Coeli; Minerva; S. M. Monserrato; Trin. Pell.—Borgia; Camera; Octagon; Rospigliosi; Villa Torlonia.

Cor. brunastra.—Brownish cement; crowded grey pebbles. *S. M. Via.*

Cor. carnina venata.—Confusion of red, pink, and white. *Scala Nobile; Statues.*

Cor. di Cori.—Dull pink and brown, shattered, and flawed with greenish grey; easily distinguished from the ancient species. *Divina Pietà; Scala Nobile.*

Cor. giallognola.—Yellow, veined with brown. *S. Giov. Lat.*

Cor. giallastra B.—Transparent, with network of brown and gold. *S. M. Maggiore.*

Cor. grande.—Markings very large. *S. Prisca.*

Cor. lionata.—Dark and bricky. *S. Lor. Lucina.*

Cor. lumacata B.—Suspicion of snails.
S. Giov. Lat.

Cor. minuta.—Very small crowded and confused pinkish white angular fragments on grey streaked ground. *Vittoria.*

Cor. min. nuvolata.—Similar, but clouded.
V. Borghese.

Cor. nuvolata.—Clouded pinkish yellow, with no visible cement. *Borghese.*

Cor. pallida.—Confused creamy white pebbles on broken lilac ground.
Gesù ; S. Giov. Lat. ; S. M. Liberatrice ; S. M. Trast.

Cor. pall. minuta.—Pinkish grey on lilac, with white streaks. *S. Ant. Port. ; S. M. Itria.*

Cor. pall. nuvolosa.—Pale pink, beautifully flushed with cloud lines of darker hue, and streaked with purple and green. *S. Giov. Fior.*

Cor. pall. venata.—Light pink, delicately veined and netted with reddish purple. *S. Sisto.*

Cor. pavonazza.—Light grey pebbles on lilac.
S. Eusebio.

Cor. pav. min.—Pebbles very small.
S. Lor. Panis.

Cor. pav. pallida.—Similar, with faint colours.
S. Lor. Fonte.

Cor. pav. scura.—Dark purple with flesh-coloured pebbles. *S. Croce.*—*Borghese.*

Cor. policroma.— Red, rose, white, and grey. Pebbles small. *S. Luigi ; S. Marco.*

Cor. rosea.—Small even stones of red, white, and grey. *Gesù ; Terme.*

Cor. rosea pallida.—Pale red, with tinge of yellow. *S. Isidoro.*

Cor. rossa.— Pinkish white, on very bright red ground rivered with purple. *S. Susanna ; Vittoria.*

Cor. rossa scura.—Cement very dark dull red, pebbles pink. *S. Lor. Fonte.*

Cor. rossa e gialla.—Yellowish pebbles on red; pebbles pink. *S. Greg. ; Hospital of S. Giov.*

Cor. rossastra dorata.—Gilded pebbles on pink. *S. M. Orto.*

Cor. schietta.—Closely set pebbles of brownish red, lilac, violet, and pink. *S. M. Orto.*

Cor. scura.— Angular grey pebbles on broken chocolate ground. *S. Dom. Sisto ; Chiesa Nuova.*

Cor. venata.—Pebbles plentifully veined with red. *Gesù.*

Cor. violacea.—Violet with pink pebbles. *S. Bibiana.*—*Stat.*

Cor. violacea dorata.—Rose, violet, and flesh colour, with patches of yellow. *S. Prassede.*

Cor. violetta giallastra.—Drab pebbles on lilac ground. *S. M. Angeli; S. P. Vincoli.*

BRECCIA DI SETTEBASI.

Settebasi bianca (see p. 24).—Almost pure white, with faint stains of blood red. *M. Torlonia.*

S. biancastra.—Pure chalky white, with veins of gold and greenish grey. *Albani.*

S. bigia.—Fine network of very pale yellow and purple, with small pebbles of dark red and grey. *S. Pietro* (Wenceslaus); *Tor de' Specchi.*

S. bigia giallastra.—Grey, with tinge of yellow. *Cap.*

S. bigia principe.—Lilac white, mapped and streaked with coast lines. *S. Stef. Rotondo;* * *S. Carlo Cat.; S. Giov. Fior.* B.

S. bruna giallastra.—Yellowish brown. *S. Stef. Rotondo.*—*Pal. Altemps.*

S. cupo.—Very dark violet. *S. Paolo.*

* **S. dorata.**—Large stones of white, pink, and grey, on chocolate ground, smeared with gold. *Ara Coeli; S. Bernardo; S. Carlo Cat.; S. Giov.*

Lat.; S. Ignazio; S. M. Minerva; Pace; Scala; Vergini; S. N. Tolentino; S. Onofrio; S. Silv. Quir.; Suffragio.

* **S. gatteggiante.**—Cream colour, clotted purple, and yellow, with blood streaks and transparent white. *S. Anastasia; S. Brigida; S. Catarina; S. Dom. Sisto.—Albani; Siciliana.*

S. gialla B.—Ivory cream, and yellow linear pebbles on rivered lilac ground.
Gesù; S. M. Vittoria; Statues.

S. mandolata.— Small pattern; almond-shaped pebbles; tinge of orange.
S. Eustachio; S. M. Angeli.

S. pavonazza.—Pinkish white, or light grey pebbles, on dark purple ground.
Chiesa Nuova; S. M. Domnica; Montesanto; Scala; S. Paolo; Suffragio.

S. pav. angolosa B.—Yellowish white and pink on chocolate. *S. M. Traspontina.*

S. pav. confusa.—Confused markings; flush of pink. *S. M. Angeli.*

S. pav. fiorita.—Very linear and minute violet and cream, flushed with gold.
S. N. Arcioni;. S. Paolo.

S. persichina B.—Yellowish brown pebbles on faint lilac. *S. Luigi.*

S. policroma.—Bright green stains on the white.
S. Clemente; S. M. Maggiore; S. Pietro (Greg.).

S. poligonia B.—Flesh-coloured white pebbles, angular in form, divided by purple lines. *B. N.*

S. rossa.—Parallel veins of rose, pink, violet, and white. *S. Pietro* (Simon and Jude).

S. rossastra.—Grey and yellow, with flush of pink. *Chiesa Nuova; S. Stef. Cacco.*

S. rossa schiacciata.—Crushed. *S. Isidoro.*

* **S. venata** (principe).—Bluish white, veined with purplish grey and netted with gold.
S. Giov. Fonte; Maddalena; Braschi.

S. verde B.—Tinge of green.
Fontana dei Termini.

S. violacea.—Grey and lilac. *S. Giov. Lat.*

BRECCIA A SEMESANTO.

Semesanto pavonazzo (see p. 24).—Sharply defined and very minute pebbles, splashed crossways with angular spots of paint.
S. Giov. Paolo; S. Lor. Lucina; S. M. Minerva; Vittoria; S. Pietro Vincoli; S. Stef. Cacco.

S. pav. minuto.—Chocolate ground, with minute pebbles of faint lilac, mostly parallel, and very closely set. A few irregularly streaked pebbles of pale pink. *S. Lor. Miranda; S. M. Maggiore.*

S. pav. pallido B.—Clouded pebbles of lilac and grey. *Egypt.*

S. giallo.—Similar in form, but brownish yellow. *S. Alessio; S. Giov. Fior.; S. M. Anima; Minerva; Vittoria; S. N. Tolentino; S. Pietro* (Confession).

Semesantone bigio.—Pebblets grey, and a little larger. *S. Agata Goti.*

S. pavonazzo. Lilac. *S. Onofrio; S. Silv. Quir.*

S. rosso.—Flushed with red. *S. Onofrio; Albani.*

BRECCIA TRACCAGNINA.

Belli calls this species *policroma*, because of its great variety of brilliant colours; but this feature is shared by so many other marbles that I have thought it best to retain the name adopted by Corsi (p. 23).

Traccagnina angolosa.—Pebbles angular. *S. Paolo.*

T. bruna dorata.—General hue, gilded brown. *S. Giov. Lat.*

T. chiara.—Colours less vivid. *Vittoria.*

T. confusa.—Markings indistinct.
S. Giov. Paolo.

T. disfatta.—Shattered ground of pinkish white; pebbles red, lilac, and striped grey. *Doria.*

T. florita.—Dark galantina with truffles, on reddish yellow clay. * *Cap.*
Cream-coloured and grey pebbles on flushed lilac. *Torlonia Corso.*

T. gialla.—Fine network of brownish yellow, enclosing tiny pebbles of transparent white, red, pink, brown, and greenish gold.
S. M. Angeli.

T. lumachellata.—Suspicion of snails. *S. Eustachio.*

T. minuta.—Markings small.
S. Sabina; S. Stanislao.

T. minuta.—Red, with small pebbles of white, pink, and violet. *S. M. Vittoria.*

T. pav. rossastra.—Pinkish purple.
S. Spirito Sassia.

T. pistacchina scura.—Dark purple, with clouded crushed pebbles of white, faint lilac, and yellowish green. *S. M. Traspontina* (3rd Chapel rt. R.).

T. policroma.—Red, pink, bluish slate, and a good deal of white. * *S. Bernardo.*

T. principe.—White, violet, greenish pink, and red, on purple ground.
S. Adriano; S. Cecilia; S. Carlo Cat.; S. Dom. Sisto; S. M. Liberatrice; S. M. Scala; S. M. Via. —Borghese.

T. principe minuta.—Grey, violet, purple, and rose.
S. Catarina; * *S. M. Orazione; S. Pudenziana; Vittoria.*

T. rossa.—Medley of red, pink, white, and bluish slate. *S. Susanna.*

* **T. rossa lumachellata.**—Pink, brown, and gilded greenish pebbles on red ground. *Terme.*

T. rossastra.—Brownish red, with a few pebbles of pure white.
Ara Coeli; Gesù.

T. rossastra.—Brick red, with grey and pink pebbles. *Chiesa Nuova.*

T. sanguigna.—Greyish brown and lilac, stained with blood red. *S. M. Popolo.*

T. violetta minuta.—Tiny pebbles on lilac ground.
S. Catarina; Monte Santo; S. Salv. Lauro.

ROSSO BRECCIATO.

MARMOR LYDIUM.—From Lydia in Asia Minor.

Rosso brecciato schietto.—Bright red, with cloudy white spots.
S. Angelo Pesch. ; S. Luigi ; S. Pietro (Confession); *S. P. Vincoli ; S. Rocco.—Cand.*

R. br. minuto.—White spots, small and rosy.
S. M. Maggiore ; Minerva ; Monti ; Traspontina ; S. Michele in Borgo.—Braschi.

R. br. bruno.—Brownish red, with white pebbles.
S. And. Quir.

R. br. confuso.—Mixed purple, violet, and white. *Altemps.*

R. br. lumachellato.—Fragments of shells.
S. Seb.

R. br. scuro.—Dark clotted purple, with tiny round pebbles of white and rose. Spots of white paint.
S. Croce.

BROCCATELLONE.†
Cream-coloured pebbles on lilac ground, tinged with yellow.

S. Agostino; S. Alessio; S. And. Valle; S. Cesareo; S. Eusebio; S. Giov. Fior.; S. Gir. Carità; S. M. Via; Minerva; S. Onofrio; S. Paolo Tre Font.; S. Tommaso in Formis.—Torlonia Corso.

Br. rosso.—Red more prominent and vivid.
Altemps.

Br. rosso e giallo.—Pale yellow and gold, with unequal pebbles of bluish rose. Pale cream on lilac, smeared with gold and purple. *Ara Coeli.*

† So called from a very superficial resemblance to *Broccatello*.

Br. giallo.—Yellow hue predominating.
S. Prassede.

Br. chiaro.—Colours very pale. *Terme.*

Br. pavonazzo.—Cream and violet pebbles on lilac ground, with flush of pinkish brown.
S. Catarina; S. M. Trast.

Occhio di Pernice.—Imitation of drab oysters,† with red eyes, on brick-red ground. Violet with lines of yellowish white, lichen of yellowish green, and inconspicuous eyes. *S. Lor. Lucina; Suffragio.*

VII. AFFRICANO.

AFFRICANO.

Marmor Chium.—From the Island of Chios. It is called African because of its dusky hue. Black, green, grey, purple, and bronze, in form of large pebbles; colours always strongly pronounced.
S. Agost.; S. Angelo Pesc.; S. Fr. Ripa; Gesù; S. Giov. Lat.; S. M. Cosm.; Consolazione; Maggiore; Tre Fontane; Trin. Pell.

Affr. bigio.—Grey, with a few stains of reddish brown. Uniform clouding of dark and light mottled grey.
S. Giac. Corso; S. Giov. Fior.; S. Pietro; Sacristy.

A. bigio fior.—Bluish grey and white, smeared with blood red. *Mus. Arch.*

† Not a shell-marble.

A. bigio scuro.—Colours all dusky and dull.
S. Salv. Lauro.
A. b. venato.—Black, sparingly veined with grey.
S. Croce Lucchesi ; S. Giov. Fonte.
A. bronzato.—Metallic hue. *SS. Nereo Ach.*
A. carnino.—Flesh coloured, in the red shades.
S. Gir. Carità.
A. corallino.—Bright coral red. *Gesù.*
A. cor. piritifero.—Black, with rose, coral red, and sulphate of iron. *Chiesa Nuova.*

A. cor. zonale.—Interrupted zones of white, grey, yellow, and vivid coral red.
S. And. Valle.—Octagon.
A. disfatto.—Crumbling to pieces.
S. Salv. Onda ; Scala Santa.
A. fiorito.—Handsome mixture of bright red, black, and purple. *S. M. Orto ; Busts.*
A. giallognolo.—Grey or greenish yellow, with marks of yellowish red. *S. Cecilia.*

A. lumacato.—Small white snails and fragments of shells. *S. Sabina.*
A. nero.—General hue black.
S. Bernardino ; SS. Nereo Ach. ; S. Pudenziana ; S. Silv. Quir.
* **A. nero brecciato.**—Jet black with pebbles of dark violet and dull crimson.
S. Apollinare ; S. Venanzio.

A. nero ondato.—Black, with greyish lines meandering between fragments of red and grey.
S. Cecilia; S. Pietro.
A. nero quarzifero.—Black, yellowish, and flesh colour, with veins of white quartz and rose.
S. Pietro.
A. nero sanguigno.—Black, with triangular patches of blood red. *Trin. Monti.*
A. pavonazzo.— Lightish grey, lilac, and rose. Dark ash, with purplish red and greyish white stains.
S. Spirito; Vittoria.—Albani.
A. pav. giallastro.—Purple, with tinge of yellow. *Suffragio.*
A. pezzato.—Piebald grey and black, with reddish pebbles. *S. Seb.*
* **A. principe.**—Black, dashed with white and pink. Tiny vivid pebbles of crimson.
Borghese; Cap.; Torlonia.
A. rosso.—Greenish brown, with large red stains, and traces of white shells.
Pantheon; S. Spirito; Vittoria.
A. rossastro. — Rosy grey with pebbles of bluish grey and spotted crimson. *S. M. Pace.*
A. rosso brecciato.—Reddish brown with angular or parallel stains of red and grey.
S. Cecilia; Temple of Concord.
A. rosso conchigliare. — Bright red rivered with grey and splashed with greyish white snails.
Vittoria.

A. rosso erborizzato.—Grey with stains of flesh colour and lichen of blood red. *S. Giov. Lat.*

A. sanguigno.—Pinkish white pebbles stained with blood red and rivered with purplish grey.
Divino Amore; S. Lor. Fonte; S. M. Maggiore; S. Pantaleo.

A. s. confuso.—Similar, but with indistinct outlines. *S. Ambrogio.*

A. schiacciato.—Smashed into fragments. *S. Pietro* (Processo).

A. venato.—Veined with white. *V. Mattei.*

A. violetto.—General hue violet.
S. Paolo Regola.

A. v. venato.—Violet, veined with white. *Cand.*

A. verde.—Bluish green with fragments of pure green and stains of flushed grey.
S. Calisto; SS. Nereo Ach.; Sacristy; S. Stef. Rotondo; Vittoria.—Mus. Torlonia.

A. v. bigiastro.—Greyish green. *Vittoria.*

A. v. lumachellato.—Bronzed green with tiny fragments of pearly shells. *S. Crisogono.*

A. v. picchiettato.—Green, punctured with black. *Octagon.*

A. v. rossastro.—Green, flushed with pink. *S. Luigi.*

VIII. ALABASTERS.
ALABASTRO ANTICO.

MARMOR ALABASTRUM.—Said to have been first brought from quarries among the Theban hermitages in Egypt, whose corrupted name it bears. Most of the following species are oriental, a few only being native. Ancient alabaster is a true marble, and differs entirely in nature and formation from the alabaster of modern science (see p. 25). Its varieties are so infinite that I have raised five of the generally accepted species to the rank of *genera*, for convenience of classification.

Al. agatino.—Very beautiful crystal white stained with rosy pink and veined with the same hues.
Stat. B.; Cap.

Al. ametista.—Pinkish white clouds edged with wavy purple in curly lines. Tinges of brown and green.
S. Lucia Gonfalone; S. Pantaleo.

Al. ametista dendritico.—Delicate lilac hue, with foliated lines of darker shade.
S. M. Maggiore; Montesanto; S. Silv. Quir.

Al. ametistino violetto.—White, beautifully foliated with purple, and tinged with yellow and red.
S. Lor. Panisperna.

Al. biancastro.—Uniform transparent bluish and faint brownish white in ribbons. *Albani.'*

Al. bianco.—Transparent gum, with light streaks of white.

S. Bibiana; S. Giov. Fonte; Sacristy.—B. N.; Borghese.

Al. bianco a nuvole.—Faint brownish white and greyish brown with chalky bluish cloud lines.
SS. Dom. Sisto; S. N. Tolentino.

Al. bianco ondato.— Highly crystallised white, with wavy lines of soiled opaque white. *Mus. Arch.*

Al. bigio dorato.—Gilded grey. *S. Catarina.*

Al. brunastro fiorito. — Brownish, flushed with rose and yellow. *S. Giov. Lat.*

Al. brunastro ondato.—Brownish, with wavy lines. *S. M. Vittoria.*

Al. bruno.—Brown. *S. Ambrogio.*

Al. bruno pallido ondato.—Light brown, with wavy lines. *S. Luca.*

Al. bruno rossastro.—Reddish brown.
Chiesa Nuova; S. Prassede.

Al. bruno rossastro listato.— Reddish brown, streaked. *Cand.*

Al. cenerino fortezzino.— Clouded grey foliated with dark grey and veined with orange and reddish brown. *S. Marco.*

* **Al. cipollino.**—Parallel lines of green, black, and pink. *Montesanto.*

Al. dorato.—Brilliant mapping of orange, violet, and pink. Mottled and foliated yellowish brown with blue and white spots.
S. Giov. Genov.; S. M. Vittoria.—Cand.

Al. eburneo.—Faint lemon white, with fine pithy wood grain. *Gesù.*

Al. fiorito.—1. Faint quince, finely striated with pink, rose, and brownish grey.
2. White, flushed with violet, mapped and circled with yellowish brown.
3. Mapping of rose, pink, and yellowish purple.
4. Pink and yellow, mottled and veined with gum.
(All the above varieties are common.)
5. Lichen of violet and gold, with veins of transparent greenish gum. *Animali.*

Al. fior. brecciato.—Rose, red, pink, and yellow, in breccia form. *Albani.*

Al. fior. giallo B.—Prevailing colour yellow.
S. Greg.

Al. fior. listato.—Close parallel veins of lilac and yellowish brown.
S. Catarina ; SS. Dom. Sisto ; Minerva.
, Vertical parallel veins of brownish red, rose, pink, and yellow. *S. Giov. Paolo ; S. Silv. Quir.*—Busts.

Al. fior. pav.—* Orange, purple, lilac, and cream colour.
Etruscan Mus.

Al. fior. melleo B.—Honey colour, flushed with pink and orange. *S. Cecilia.*

Al. fior. muscoso B.—Mossy. *S. And. Valle.*

Al. fior. spezzato B.—Shattered rose, pink, yellow, and white. *S. Giac. Corso.*

Al. fior. venato.—1. Lichen of pinkish brown, with broad streaks of yellow.

2. Veined rose and yellow.

3. Brownish red, yellow, and pinkish white. (All these are common.)

Al. fortezzino. — Transparent gum and wavy islands of chalky white edged with light brown.

S. Carlo Cat.; SS. Dom. Sisto; S. Ignazio.

Rosy white streaked with pure white and yellowish brown.

S. M. Maggiore; Vittoria; S. Rocco.

Al. fort. lumachellato B.—Zigzag markings of white and brownish grey. Suspicion of shells.

Gesù; Vittoria.

Al. fort. occhiuto.—Light quince, zigzagged with chalky white, light brown, and grey.

S. Martino.

Al. a giaccione.—Transparent white, with texture of sugar candy.

S. Lor. Borgo B.; *Altieri; Borghese; Busts; Cap.*

Al. a giaccione rossastro.—Similar, with flush of pink. *Cand.*

Al. giallastro nuvolato.—Clouded yellow.

Chiesa Nuova.

Al. giallo brecciato.—Yellow, with blotches resembling pebbles. *S. Anastasia.*
Al. giallo fiorito.—Yellow, flushed with red. *Cand.*
Al. giallo listato.—Narrow bands of pink, violet, lilac, white, and brown.
Annunziata ; S. Catarina ; Gesù Maria.—Borghese.
Al. giallognolo.—Brownish yellow, clouded with lighter shade.
S. And. Valle ; Albani ; Barberini.

Al. listato.—Parallel lines of pink, brown, white, and yellow. *Cand.*
Al. listato verdiccio.—Similar, with greenish hue. *Scuola Castigliana.*

* **Al. marino.**—Transparent brownish white with lines of pure opaque white, and hair strokes of purple and yellowish brown.
S. And. Valle ; Gesù ; S. Cecilia.
Al. marino dorato.—Gilded. *S. M. Popolo.*

Al. melleo.—Uniform pale brownish yellow, finely mottled and dotted with black.
Albani.
Al. melleo cupo (listato).—Petrified fine maple grain, with parallel veins. *S. Dorotea.*
Al. melleo fiorito (di rosa).—Honey-coloured, with flush of rose.
S. Isidoro ; SS. Nereo Ach. ; S. Sabina.

Al. melleo listato.—Honey-coloured, finely striated with pink, rose, and grey.
S. Catarina ; S. Lor.—Borghese ; Cand.
* **Al. melleo nuvolato.**—Honey-coloured, with cloud lines of purple.
S. M. Maggiore ; Quattro Coron.
* **Al. melleo rossiccio.**—Bright orange mottled with pinkish brown, pink and honey.
S. M. Traspontina ; S. Pietro (Girolamo).
Al. a nuvole.—Snow-white patched with lemon and mapped with curved parallel veins of transparent white and brown, bordered with cords of light brown.
S. Marco ; Vittoria ; S. Pietro (Confession).
Al. nuvolato bruno.—Brown, with cloud lines.
S. Vitale.

Al. occhiuto.—White and grey, with concentric mappings of yellow, rose, and white.
Gesù ; S. Carlo Cat. ; S. Lor. in Lucina ; S. Rocco.
Al. ad onice.—Grey, pink, violet, and white.
S. Catarina ; S. Carlo Cat. ; Minerva ; Scala ; Vittoria.
Al. onichino.—Grey and opaque white, slightly zigzag.
S. Croce ; Gesù Maria ; S. Ignazio ; S. P. Vincoli ; S. Prassede ; S. Pietro (Confession).*—Cand.*
Al. onichino fiorito.—Similar, with flush of yellow.
Trin. Pell.
Al. onichino rossastro.—Similar, with flush of pink. *Cand.*

Al. orientale oleoso B.—Yellow and cream in many shades. *S. Salv. Lauro.*

Al. pav. occhiuto.—Lilac, with circlets. *S. Catarina.*

Al. perlaceo B.—Pearly transparent white, with parallel veins of gum. *S. Giov. Fonte.*

Al. pomato.—Brownish white, with clouds of whiter hue and streaks of brown. *S. Clemente; S. Susanna.*

Al. a rosa.—Pale yellow blotched with pink and white. *Vittoria; S. P. Vincoli; S. Pudenziana; S. Silv. Quir.—Borghese.*

Al. a rosa carnicino.—Raw beef; parallel veins of dark red and yellow. *S. Cecilia* (corniolino).

Al. a rosa cinabrino fasciato B.R.—Parallel veins of red, orange, white, and yellow. † *Gesù.*

* **Al. a rosa confuso.**—Blotches of rose, ill-defined in outline. *S. Onofrio.*

Al. a rosa dendritico.—Red, with marks like the outline of a tree. *S. Seb.*

Al. a rosa fiorito.—Roundish handsome blotches and veins of crimson. *S. M. Maggiore.*

Al. a rosa giallo.—Bright yellow blotched with rose. *S. Gregorio.*

Al. a rosa listato.—Bands of flaky transparent

† Probably a jasper.

white edged with gold, and opaque white flushed with rose.

S. And. Valle; S. Catarina; Vittoria.—Cap.
Narrow bands of rose, pink, lilac, violet, and transparent grey. *S. And. Valle.*

Al. a rosa nuvolato dorato.—Mottled red and white, foliated with orange. *Ara Coeli; S. Cecilia.*

Al. a rosa ranciato.—Fine parallel streaks of very opaque coral and white. *S. Pietro* (Madonna).

Al. a rosa sfrangiato.—Bands of white with interrupted rose marks. *S. And. Valle; Cand.*

* **Al. a rosa venato.**—Veined rose colour. *S. Onofrio.*

Al. rosso.—Clouded white and cinnabar pink. *Gesù; S. Silv. Quir.—Borghese.*

Al. rosso fortezzino.—Two shades of red, spots of white, and blotches of orange. *S. Lor. Fonte.*

Al. rosso nuvolato.—Clouded red. *S. Spirito.*

Al. rosso e giallo.—Dark yellow spotted and patched with rose.
Ara Coeli; S. Giov. Lat.; S. Salv. Lauro; S. Pietro (Sebastiano).

Al. rosso e giallo listato.—Red and yellow in parallel lines.
S. Croce Lucchesi; S. Michele Borgo; S. Silv. Quir.

Al. rossastro.—Very fine flaky mottled violet, pink, and rose. *S. M. Angeli.*

Al. rossastro venato.—Pinkish, with veins of red, violet, and yellow. *Doria.*

Al. rossiccio.—Narrow bands of rose, pink, violet, and transparent grey. *Ara Coeli.*

Al. venato.—Crystallised flaky white veined with red and brown. *Chiaramonti.*

Al. verde giallognolo.—Greenish gum flushed with reddish yellow, and full of crystal. *Cap.*

A v. listato.—Highly crystallised flaky uniform greenish white. *S. Catarina.*

Al. verdognolo.—Uniform transparent pale greenish gum, tinged with pink and yellow. *S. Agnese fuori; Busts.*

A. v. cupo B.—Similar, but darker green. *Cap.*

A. v. chiaro B.—Green very faint and transparent. *B. N.; Cap.*

Al. violetto listato.—Shades of violet, in narrow stripes. *S. Croce.*

MODERN SPECIES.

Al. di Civitavecchia.—Streaked in wavy lines of pink and light brown, plentifully knotted with pure white. Rather coarse. *S. Onofrio; Cand.*

Striated brown, red, and yellow, with faint spots of white. *S. Eligio.—Busts.*

Al. di Karnak.—Yellow, close grained; sometimes stained with red, mottled white, or spotted with brown. *Egypt.*

Al. di Montauto.—Brown in various shades, finely

striated and mottled, with general appearance of petrified timber.
S. Crisogono; S. Silv. Quir.—Borghese.

Al. di Montauto nuvolato.—Similar, but clouded. *Stimmate.*

Al. del Monte Circeo.—Brownish, veined; here and there patched with gummy white. *Masks.*

* **Al. di Orte.**—Sugar candy.
S. Pietro (Confession); *Busts; Cand.*

ALABASTRO COTOGNINO.

Cotognino arancio.—Whity-brown flushed with orange and lined with chalky white or yellowish brown. *S. Claudio.*

C. arancio listato.—Streaked orange. *Cand.*

C. bianco.—Uniform transparent white. *Library.*

C. bianco listato.—Transparent white, with narrow bands. *Borghese.*

C. bianco venato.—Veined transparent white. *Cand.*

C. chiaro.—Similar, but more transparent. *S. Ignazio.*

C. cupo.—Dark quince. *Borghese.*

C. dendritico.—Dark grey lichen on mottled gum. *S. And. Valle.*

C. listato.—Narrow lines of chalky white. *Borghese.*

C. a nuvole.—Quince lined with chalky white.
S. M. Angeli; S. Silv. Quir.; S. Venanzio.

C. principe.—Brownish yellow, mottled and honey-combed, with streaks and patches of chalky white.
S. Benedetto; S. Lor. Fuori; S. Lor. Damaso; S. M. Maggiore; S. Paolo; Trin. Monti.

C. venato.—Chalky-white sago and light gum, veined with pink.
S. N. Carcere; S. Paolo.—Statues.

C. verdiccio.—Light green transparent gum, tinged with yellow. *Cap.*

ALABASTRO DI PALOMBARA.

Named from a Villa outside the Porta Pia where it was first found. It always contains more or less of solid opaque white.

Palombara bianco listato.—Pure chalky white, finely ribboned with yellowish brown.
S. Bernardo.

Pal. brunastro.—Lichen of pinkish brown, mapped and waved with light brown and bordered with dark lines. *S. Carlo Cat.*

Pal. dendritico.—Parallels of opaque ivory or bluish white, violet, and pinkish brown.
S. Fr. Ripa; S. Paolo; S. Spirito.

Pal. eburneo.—Ivory white. *S. Isidoro.*

Pal. fasciato.—Broad band of ivory veined with delicate strokes of pink and brown.
S. M. Traspontina; S. Prassede.

Pal. listato.—Fine parallel lines of brown, pink, lilac, and green. Colours dull. Common. *S. Pietro.*

Pal. listato fiorito.—Light brown, with islands of darker shade and chocolate coast line. *S. Lor. Lucina.*

Pal. pavonazzo.—Striated lilac, yellowish brown, and white. *Pantheon.*

Pal. rigato.—Similar, with lines more decided and firm. *Trin. Pell.*

Pal. rossastro.—Pinkish brown lichen, veined with opaque white. *S. Gius. Capo le Case.*

Pal. rosso listato.—Straight parallel lines of chalky white, light brown, and gum. Part mottled with pink lichen. *S. N. Tolentino.*

Pal. tartarugato B.—Opaque white, with foliage of tortoise-shell. *S. Catarina.*

Pal. violetto.—Light chalky violet with veins and cross lines of earthy brown.
S. Giac. Corso; Vittoria.

ALABASTRO SARDONICO.

* **Sardonico bianco.**—Very light hue. *S. Alessio.*

Sard. bruno.—Opaque purple and yellowish brown. *Animali.*

Sard. chiaro.—Transparent gum. *S. Onofrio.*

Sard. giallo e rosso.—Glue, tinged with yellow and red. *S. Pudenziana.*

Sard. listato.—Glue and gum, in wavy lines. *S. Catarina ; Vittoria.*

Sard. macchiato.—Light mottled brown gum spotted with chalky white. *SS. Dom. Sisto.*

Sard. nuvolato.—Clouded. *S. M. Montesanto.*

Sard. occhiuto chiaro.—Glue, with large eyes of lighter shade. *S. Giov. Paolo.*

Sard. ondato.—Mottled toffy brown with wavy streaks of lighter hue.
S. And. Valle ; SS. Dom. Sisto.

Sard. pomato.—Mottled gum and glue.
S. Ignazio.

Sard. a rosa.—Tinge of pink, in pools.
S. M. Popolo ; Mus. Torlonia.

Sard. a rosa nuvolato.—Tinge of pink, in clouds. *S. Ignazio ; S. M. Maggiore ; Umiltà.*

Sard. scuro.—Dark sugar candy glue and transparent gum.
S. Martina ; S. P. Vincoli ; S. Seb.

* **Sard. tartarugato agatino.**—Glue, with irregular tortoise-shell markings. *S. Calisto.*

S. t. giallo.—Veined rose and yellow. *Animali.*

Sard. tartarugato scuro.— Dark coffee brown, slightly veined.
S. And. Valle; SS. Dom. Sisto.

ALABASTRO A TARTARUGA.

Tartaruga brunastro.— Oblique parallel veins; three shades of brown. R.
S. Greg.; S. Gir. Carità; Scala Santa.
T. florito.— Finely lichened violet, brown, or white, on yellow or lilac. *S. Catarina; S. Marco.*
T. giallastro. — Yellowish brown veined and lichened with violet and greyish red.
S. M. Vittoria; Borghese.
T. giallo e rosso.—Veins of brownish yellow and mottled pinkish brown.
S. M. Liberatrice; Scala; S. Rocco.—Cap.
T. listato.—Minutely striated yellowish brown and purple, with streaks of faint brown lichen.
S. And. Valle; S. Cat. Funari.
T. pallido.—Pale tortoise-shell. *Vittoria.*
T. pallido occhiuto.—Similar, with small eyes.
S. Isidoro.
T. rigato.—Tortoise-shell, in parallel lines.
S. Lor. in Lucina.
T. rosso.—Tortoise-shell, with red tinge. *S. Marco.*

ALABASTRO A PECORELLA.

Pecorella carnino B.—Flesh colour.
Octagon (in part).

P. dorato.—Flushed pinkish white patched with lichen of dark red, slightly tinged with gold.
Octagon (in part).
P. listato.—Disposition to parallel lines.
S. Salv. Lauro.
P. minuto.—Fleecy mottling very fine and even.
S. Pietro (Petronilla).
P. min. nuvolato.—Clouded fleece, small in texture.
S. Cecilia.
P. pallido.—Pale fleecy marks.
S. M. Traspontina.
P. a rosa.—Bands of rosy transparent white mixed with fleecy mottlings.
Agonizzanti ; Minerva ; S. Paolo Tre Fontane ; S. P. Vincoli.
P. sanguigno.—Flush of blood red.
S. Giac. Corso.

IX. JASPERS, AGATES, AND PRECIOUS STONES.

JASPIS.—The Romans obtained jasper from Scythia, Cyprus, and Egypt, but there is very little left of their importation. Though exceedingly difficult to define, true jasper may be easily recognised by the hard solid texture and well-defined colours of its surface, which is always more or less veined or circled with some transparent stone, usually agate. The only other marble with which it can be confounded is ancient alabaster, which always betrays at once its stalagmitic formation.

Very beautiful fragments of jasper are occasionally found on the *gradino* of a rich altar, or among the decorations of its tabernacle.

Sicilian jasper does not in the least resemble the marble after which it is named, and is for the most part very coarse and gaudy.

ACHATES.—Corsi describes twelve species of agate, but gives only two examples for identification, which I have retained. The name is derived from a river in Sicily, near which the mineral was first found. Tiny bits of agate may sometimes be found among the richly veined alabasters.

A few other stones are mentioned on the authority of Corsi, and because he gives an example of them; but they do not properly form any part of our present subject.

Diaspro giallo.—Patches of yellow, in various shades.

S. M. Scala ; Scuola Castigliana.

D. infimo.—Pale pink, with a good deal of flint grey and white, and bluish flaws.

S. Marco ; S. Pietro.

D. Lisimaco.—Dark greenish black, blotched with gold, and a few spots of blue. * *Cand.*

D. listato.—Veined crimson, pink, and white.

S. And. Valle.

D. pavonazzo.—Patches of purple. *Minerva.*

D. rosso.—Brilliant crimson, mapped with duller tints. *S. Martino.*

D. r. venato.—Bright red, veined with white and transparent blue. * *Cand.*

D. r. brecciato.—Crimson, with patches of pink or yellowish red, like pebbles.
Minerva : S. Paolo.

D. rosso dendritico.—Red, with lines resembling foliage. *Vittoria.*

D. r. e giallo.—Crimson, mapped and streaked with yellow. *S. M. Itria.*

D. r. e verde.—Red and green in blotches, stained with crystal white. *Cand.*

D. r. listato.—Crimson, with parallel bands. *S. Stef. Rotondo.*

D. tenero di Sicilia.—Red, unburnt brick colour, and a little green.
SS. Dom. Sisto; S. Pietro.

D. t. conchigliare.—The same, densely crowded with small white snails, each of which has a brownish red eye. *S. Ant. Port.; SS. Dom. Sisto.*

D. verdastro rigato.—Greenish, with finely drawn bands. *S. Pietro* (Sebastiano).

D. verde.—Yellowish green.
S. N. Tolentino; S. Stef. Cacco; S. Stef. Rotondo.

D. v. e giallo.—Green and yellow. *S. Sabina.*

Legno pietrificato.—Many shades of green, brown, and yellow, in parallel bands like timber grain.
* *S. M. Maggiore.*

L. p. verde.—Similar, with green as the prevailing hue. *Vittoria*.

Agata cotognina.—Pure transparent quince. *Library*.

A. rossa.—Brilliant red. *Vittoria*.

A. zaffirina.—Transparent bluish white. *Kirch. Mus.*

Corniola.— Semi-transparent, with hue of pomegranate. *Kirch. Mus.*

Cristallo iridato.—Sparkling white (rock-crystal). *Sacristy.—Library*.

Niccolo.— White agate, surrounded by a ring of reddish brown. *Kirch. Mus.*

Pietra di Labradore.—From the Island of St. Paul, off the coast of Labrador in Newfoundland. It is chiefly composed of feldspar, in translucent flakes.

Dark mottled blue and brown, with metallic hue of shot silk on the surface, displaying beautiful colours.
* *Library*.

LAPIS LAZZULI.

Lapis Cyanus.— A silicate of soda, lime, and alumina, with probably sulphate of iron and sodium. When powdered and washed it becomes *Ultramarine*. The best kinds are said to be found in Scythia and China.

Bright blue, with pools and streaks of lighter shade *Gesù*.

Lapis Lazzuli macchiato.—Surface broken into irregular patches of white.
S. Catarina; S. Pietro Vincoli.
L. l. scuro.—Very dark blue—almost black.
S. Paolo.

MALACHITE.

Molochites.—Green carbonate of copper, formed by a cupriferous solution which has deposited its residue in a stalagmitic form. The ancients obtained it from Arabia and China, but it is now found in Sweden and Siberia.

Bright green, mapped in concentric circles and other figures. *S. Paolo.*

PLASMA DI SMERALDO.

Smaragdus Cyprius.—From Cyprus; also found sparingly in the Tyrol. Semi-transparent mottled bluish grey, with flaws of chalky white.
S. And. delle Fratte; S. And. Valle.

SPATO FLUORE ANTICO.

Murrha.—Used for making cups by the Romans, and very highly esteemed. It was brought chiefly from Parthia.

Pale yellow, fringed with greyish green, on a ground of violet, white, and azure.
Gesù; S. M. Maggiore; S. Pietro.
S. f. listato.—Similar, but banded. *S. Onofrio.*

X. ARENACEOUS AND CALCAREOUS STONES.

Calcarea bigia.—Chalky white, with numerous grey fragments resembling snails.
S. Marco; S. Pietro; S. Crisogono; Gesù e Maria.

Calcarea gialliccia di Egitto. B.—Yellowish white, with marks of tawny jasper. *Egypt.*

Arenaria gialla di Egitto. B.—Yellow with brilliant white spots (Avventurina). *Egypt.*

A. rossa di Egitto. B.—Blood red, with a few tiny stains of white. *Egypt.*

XI. SERPENTINES.

SERPENTINA COMUNE.

MARMOR LIGUSTICUM, so called because some of the handsomest kinds are found in the province of Liguria. Several of these bear a strong superficial resemblance to granite.

Serp. bigia.—Dark green, covered with fine network of pinkish white, and streaked with pure white. *Cand.*

Serpentina brecciata nera.—Yellowish green with small angular fragments of greenish brown.
S. Giov. Fonte.

S. fiorita.—Purple streaked with white. *S. Silv. Quir.*

S. granatifera.—Greenish grey with metallic rose spots, or ruby spots edged with transparent olive green. *Cand.; Kirch. Mus.*

[Brownish green tending to grey, with crystals of granite. B.]

S. bigia verdastra.—Two shades of semi-transparent olive green, with metallic chips. *Cand.*

S. moschinata verde.—Dark green streaked with light green and stained with greenish or pinkish yellow. *S. Salv. Lauro.*

Serp. pav.—Violet, fringed with pale green and streaked with pure white. A few spots of black. *Cand.*

Serp. reticolata dell' Elba.—Greenish veins on dark purple. *Chiaramonti.*

Dark green netted with light green and pinkish white. *S. Giov. Lat.*

Serp. tigrata.—Very dark green lichened with pure fleecy white and transparent green. *S. Pantaleo.*

Serp. verde e pav.—Green scratched with purple. *Cand.*

Serp. violacea.—Ashy violet with white veins. *Minerva.*

Serp. di Genova.—Olive and light green; metallic. *Cand.*

Serp. di Tebe (*Thebes*).—Light green scrawled with purple, and flawed with veins. *Cand.*

VERDE DI PONSEVERA.

Green, veined and netted with pinkish white. (From *Ponsevera*, near Genoa.) *Cand.*

Metallic green, streaked with white and finely netted with green. *Albani.*

Bluish green on lighter shade, mixed with white. *S. M. Monserrato.*

V. di P. chiaro.—Streams of very light green and black. *S. Cat. Funari ; S. Onofrio ; Via Lata.*

ROSSO DI LEVANTO.

From the Italian Riviera, between Spezia and Genoa. Dark mottled red and black, with a few green pebbles; all streaked and rivered with white.
S. Crisogono; S. Lucia Gonfalone; S. Rocco.—Lat. Mus.; Terme.

VERDE RANOCCHIA.

LAPIS OPHITES.—Ophite appears to have been a general term for all Serpentines, because of their snake-like hue. Two species of *Verde ranocchia* were called LAPIS AUGUSTEUS and L. TIBERIANUS, because brought from Egypt in the time of Augustus and Tiberius respectively, but it is not certain which of the following were thus imported. It is found at *St. Tropez* and other places on the French Riviera.

Verde ranocchia fibroso.—Greenish yellow and dark green with fibres of pearly grey like tufts of hair.
S. Luigi ; Animali.

V. r. giallastro.—Yellowish hue. *Egypt.*

V. r. lineare.—Parallel hair lines of black in lineal network, on ground of light green in several shades.
Conservatori ; Egypt.

V. r. macchiato.—Green, with stains of metallic black. *S. Stef. Cacco; Cand.*

V. r. ondato.—Wavy light and dark green, with a little white. *S. Spirito; Animali.*

V. r. orbicolare.—Covered with tiny circles. *S. M. Anima; S. Agata dei Goti.*—Egypt.

V. r. scuro.—Hair streaks of dark green on lighter shade. *S. N. Tolentino.*

V. r. chiaro.—Very light green. *Ludovisi.*

VERDE DI PRATO.

From the hills above Prato. Largely employed on the outside of the Cathedral at Florence, and in several Churches. Olive black, spotted with dark green. *Animali.*

VERDE ANTICO.

LAPIS ATRACIUS.—First brought by the Romans from Atrax in Thessaly. Though a true serpentine, it ranks as a *Serpentina Nobile* for the handsome disposition of its markings and the purity of its colours (see p. 30), which are due to the presence of limestone.

Verde antico.—Light green with fragments of dark green, blue, black, and white.

S. Alessio; S. Carlo Cat.; Chiesa Nuova; Gesù; S. Giov. Decollato; S. Luigi; S. M. Pace.—Arazzi; Conservatori.

Verde biancastro minuto.—Pale green, with small markings. *S. Lor. fuori.*

V. chiaro.—Very light green, rushing like a torrent over spots and pebbles of darker hue.
S. M. Monticelli; S. Sabina; S. Bernardo; S. Greg.—Doria.

V. cipollino.—Greyish green, and dirty white, with a few fragments of black. *S. Brigida.*

V. cupo.—Very dark green.
Ara Coeli; Minerva.

V. mandolato.—Disposition almond-shaped.
S. Giov. Lat.

V. minuto.—Dark green with tiny fragments of black and blue, but no white. *Minerva.*

V. ondato.—Wavy green and white, between fragments of oblong black. *S. And. Valle.*

V. pallido.—Pale green.
S. Giac. Corso; S. M. Maggiore; S. Seb.—Cand.

V. pallido brecciato.—Pale green and white, evenly distributed. *S. M. Consolazione.*

V. pallido minuto.—Pale green, with small markings. *S. Pietro.*

V. picchiettato.—Dark green, punctured with black.
S. Giov. Paolo; Scala Santa; S. Sabina; Vittoria.

* **V. principe.**—Green and white both very pure.
S. Clemente; Animali.
V. sanguigno.—Stains of blood red. Rospigliosi.
V. scuro.—Dusky green. S. Agnese Navona.

V. smeraldo.—Emerald green. Minerva.

Verde di Firenze.—Greyish green with faint streaks of brown, and white stains.
S. Ambrogio; S. Apollinare; S. Croce; S. Pudenziana.—V. Albani.
Verde di Grecia.—Uniform greyish green with streaks of fleecy white. From rediscovered quarries in Greece.
S. Giov. Paolo; S. Paolo; S. Rocco; S. Salv. Onda.
Verde di Susa.—Dull green, with very little impure white, and a few black stains.
S. And. Valle; S. Cat. Funari; S. Seb.

PIETRA NEFRITICA.

Lapis Aequipondus.—(See p. 31.) Jet black, minutely dusted with grey; metallic texture.
S. Lor.; S. M. Trast.—Cap. (p. 31).
Pietra nefritica bronzina.—Dark metallic brown, with suspicion of grey dust.
S. M. Cosmedin; S. Martino.
P. n. bruna.—Dusky brown. Metallic spots barely visible. S. Sabina; Scala Coeli.

P. n. nera.—Jet black. *Lat. Mus.*
P. n. verde.—Dark green, with tiny spots of lighter hue. *S. Cosma.*

AMIANTO.

Lapis Amiantus.—A stone nearly allied to the Serpentines, and of so singular a flexibility that the Romans are said to have made shrouds of it, for wrapping round the bodies burnt on a funeral pyre, so that the ashes of the dead might not mingle with those of the fuel. The colour may be white, yellowish, or grey, and very rarely green or red. There is an example in the *Vat. Library.*

XII. PORPHYRY.

Lapis Porphyrites.—Common in many parts of Europe, and always imparting a warm rich colour to the cliffs and ravines where it is found; but the best of the modern kinds, when examined in detail and polished for ornamental purposes, are vastly inferior both in texture and brilliancy to those imported from Egypt by the Romans.

Porfido rosso.—Very dark reddish purple, crowded with small pinkish spots.

S. Adriano; S. Bartol.; S. Carlo Cat.; S. Eustachio; Gesù; S. Giov. Lat.; S. Greg.; S. Marcello; S. Marco; S. M. Domnica; S. M. Maggiore; Trastevere; SS. Nereo Ach.; S. Pancrazio; S. Pantaleo; S. Paolo; S. Pietro (Baptistery); *S. P. Vincoli; S. Prassede;*

Scala Santa.—*Arazzi; Borghese; Conservatori; Sala Rotonda.*

P. r. chiaro (ubbriaco).—Colour very bright, inclining to pink.
Cand.

P. r. confuso.—Pink spots very much crowded and confused. *S. Giov. Fonte ; S. Crisogono.*

P. r. cupo. B.—Darkish red with rosy white and a few black crystals. *Pantheon.*

P. r. laterizio. R.—Brick red, spotted with pink and transparent white. A few spots of black. *Albani.*

P. r. lattinato B.—Chocolate with milk white crystals, evenly distributed. *S. Agnese fuori.—Cap.*

P. pavonazzo. B.—Dark purple with even crystals of milky white. *S. Giov. dei Genov.; S. Lor. fuori.*

P. r. pomato.—Blood red with crystals of rose and black and patches of greyish green.
SS. Cosma Damiano ; S. Lor. fuori.—Octagon.

P. r. porporino.—Blood red with many crystals of lighter red and a few white.
Croce Greca ; Cand.

***P. r. scuro plasmato.**—Dark red, with patches of light green. *S. Giov. Fonte.*

Porfido verde.—Olive green, with many little crystals of yellowish green and larger ones of white.
Ara Coeli ; S. N. Carcere ; S. Saba.—Mus. Arch.

Dark green, spotted with pale greyish green. *Animali ; Borghese ; Cand. ; Mus. Arch.*

P. v. dorato.—Tinge of gold. *Albani.*

Porfido bigio.—Bluish, with even crystals of quartz or bluish or whitish feldspar, and others blacker and smaller.

S. Pietro (Greg.).—*Octagon; Lat. Mus.; Mus. Arch.; Piazza S. M. Pianto ; Terme.*

P. b. turchiniccio. R.—Similar, with bluish tinge. *V. Albani.*

P. b. rossastro.—Pinkish. *Cand.*

* **Porfido nero.**—Black, slightly tending to green, with little white crystals.

Mus. Arch. ; Scala Nobile ; Terme.

* **P. n. grafico.** B.—Oblong white or greenish crystals and tiny lumps of milky quartz, akin to agate or chalcedony. *S. Saba.*

PORFIDO SERPENTINO.

LAPIS LACEDAEMONIM.—From Laconia, in the Peloponnesus. Inferior qualities are, however, found in abundance elsewhere. For the important distinction between *Porfido Serpentino* and *Serpentina*, see p. 33.

Serpentina is a noun substantive, the generic name of a large group of serpentines ; *Serpentino* is an adjective, merely appended to *Porfido* as descriptive of some of its varieties.

Porfido serpentino verde.—Dark green with crossed crystals (others star-like, in lighter green), and white quartz.

S. Giov. Fonte; S. M. Maggiore; S. Tommaso Cenci; S. P. Vincoli.—Animali.

P. s. verde agatato.—Spots of chalcedony instead of white quartz.

S. Cesareo; Cand. (violet crystals).

P. s. verde bruno. B.—Brown with green crystals and many spots and veins of chalcedony and corniola. *S. Lor. Fuori.*

P. serp. verde cupo.—Dark green, spotted black, with Chinese letters of light green.

S. Giov. Fonte; S. Lor. Fuori; S. Paolo.

P. s. bigio R. (nero B.).—Black, with greenish grey crystals and cross crystals of light grey.

S. Prassede.—Cand.; Mus. Arch.

XIII. GRANITE.

This is not a marble, but a crystallised granular rock usually composed of black *mica*, white *quartz*, and *feldspar* in many shades of pink, violet, or grey. It takes a high polish, and its general hue is determined by the predominance of one or another of the above constituents, which however, in the commoner kinds, are pretty evenly distributed (see p. 33). Granite bears very much the same relation to coloured marble as the grasses bear to coloured flowers; and just as the advanced Student of Nature will frequently take even more pleasure in examining a spike or panicle than a corolla, so will the traveller, who has learnt to admire the most beautiful specimens of ancient Alabaster or Breccia, turn aside with still greater interest to inspect minutely a column or slab of Granite, wherein the ordinary observer can discern nothing more remarkable than a surface of dull drab or grey.

GRANITO ROSSO.

LAPIS PYRRHOPOECILUS.—From Syene (Assouan), and thence called *Syenite* (see p. 33).

Crystals of fiery red, mixed with black, white and green.

S. Costanza ; S. M. Cosm. ; S. Pietro ; Sacristy ; S. Sisto.—Obelisk of the *Pantheon, Pincio,* and *Piazza Navona ; Octagon ; Scala Nobile.*

Granito rosso fasciato. R.—Red, banded with grey. *S. M. Trast.*

Gr. rosso macchiato. B.—Mixture of red and black granite in patches.

S. Crisogono : Obelisk of *M. Citorio.*

Gr. rosso minuto.—Red, with very small markings. *Terme.*

Gr. rosso pallido.—Pale red.

S. Croce ; Croce Greca.

Gr. rosso verdastro.—Greenish hue in the feldspar. *S. M. Maggiore.*

Gr. rosso verdognolo.—Greenish red. *Egypt.*

Gr. rosso violaceo.—Red, with violet hue. *S. M. Cosm.*

Gr. rosso delle Guglie. B.—Large rosy crystals with smaller ones of yellowish white and black.
Obelisk of the *Piazza Minerva, Vatican,* and *V. Mattei.*

Gr. rossastro.—Pink. *S. Pietro* (Petronilla).

Gr. rossastro tigrato.—Pink, with pools of grey, at even distances. *Cand.*

Gr. roseo.—Vivid rosy red.
Obelisk of the *Lateran.*

Gr. roseo fasciato. B.—Rose, yellowish white, and black, banded or stained with small red and black crystals, evenly distributed. *S. Crisogono.*

Gr. roseo minuto. B.—Rose, with tiny chips of black mica. *Cand.*

GRANITO DEL FORO.

White quartz and feldspar with black spots of mica equally distant, and a few yellowish dots. B.

S. Alessio; S. Costanza; S. Giov. Port. Lat.; S. M. Cosm.; S. M. Maggiore; Pantheon; S. Pietro; Sacristy.—Forum of Trajan; B. N.; Octagon; Scala Nobile.

LAPIS PSARONIUS.—So called because spotted like a starling. It is supposed to have been first brought by Trajan from Syene (Assouan) for the columns of his

Forum and its enclosures, and its presence in the portico of the Pantheon has furnished an interesting argument for the true date of that building (*Handbook*, Rte. 16).

Granito del Foro bicolore.—Similar, banded with red. *S. M. Trast.*

Gr. del Foro roseo. B.—Rosy, with spots and veins of grass green. *Pantheon.*

Gr. del Foro arrugginito.—Rusted with chocolate or bronze. *S. Pietro* (M. della Colonna). *Borghese.*

GR. BIGIO.

Lapis Syenites, from Syene.

Black, with minute lichen of grey, and tinge of pinkish brown.

S. Giov. Lat.; S. Lazzaro; S. Pancrazio; S. Pietro; S. Prassede; S. Sisto; SS. Vincenzo ed Anast. (Tre Fontane).

V. Albani; Scala Nobile.

Gr. bigio bronzato.—Dark grey, with short faint black lines, and spots of coppery mica. *Farnese.*

Gr. b. cupo tigrato.—Dark grey, with lighter pools. *Cand.*

Gr. b. dendritico.—Foliated like the branch of a tree. *Cand.*

Gr. b. macchiato.—Grey, spotted with white. *Cand.*

Gr. b. minuto.—Minute mixture of black, white, and pink, like grey cloth.
S. Greg.; Etruscan Mus.

Gr. bigio minuto confuso. R.—Dark bluish grey with lichen of lighter shade, indistinctly traced.
Ara Coeli.

G. b. m. lineare.—Similar, with disposition to lines.
Cand.

G. b. m. rossastro.—Similar, with suspicion of pink.
P. Grazioli.

G. b. m. rossiccio. R.—Mottled drab, with a hue of pink over all. *Egypt.*

Gr. bigio perlato. B.—Black dots and white spots on pearly grey. *Borghese.*

G. b. rossastro.—Similar, with hue of pink.
Croce Greca.

G. b. terreo. B.—Whitish earthy grey sown with spots of black. *S. Giorgio.*

G. b. turchiniccio.—Greyish lilac, with foliation of white, and spots of black. *Egypt.*

Gr. b. verdastro.—Greenish grey. *Borghese.*

Gr. bigio e nero.—Bluish grey on jet black. *Cand.*

G. b. verdognolo. B. (pedicolare).—Small oblong whitish and black crystals on greenish grey. *Cand.*

Gr. bruno minuto.—Brown, with small markings.
S. M. Maggiore.

Gr. bruno giallastro. B.—Sooty brown with minute round light spots like transparent gems.
S. Agata dei Goti.

Gr. carnicino grigiastro. B.—Marbled with flesh colour, pale grey, and black. *S. Spirito.*

Gr. corallino minuto. B.—Minute mixture of fiery red, and reddish black. *Kirch. Mus.*

Gr. dendritico (erborizzato S.).—Lilac and white ground, with foliation of black. *S. Pietro.*

G. di Giglio.—From the Island of Giglio in the Mediterranean. Grey, with large crystallised lilac spots. *S. Anastasia ; S. Croce.*

G. di Giglio macchiato.—Similar, with stains of black and white. *S. M. Maggiore.*

Gr. persichino.—Grey, plentifully flushed with lilac. Some of it is modern, and comes from Sardinia.
S. Costanza ; S. Giorgio ; S. Martino ; S. Pietro ; S. Prisca.—B. N.; Albani; Etruscan Mus.; Papa Giulio ; Scala Nobile.

Gr. tigrato.—Dark greenish grey, with even pools of lighter grey. *Chiaramonti.*

Gr. tigrato bianco. B.—Minute mixture of black, pink, and green, with here and there a spot of white feldspar. *S. Giov. Lat.—Animali.*

Gr. tigrato rosso. B.—Red, plentifully spotted with black, and stained with greyish or flesh-coloured green. *Egypt.*

Gr. tigrato verde B.—Greenish black, with spots of green and rose. *Egypt.*

Gr. tigrato verdognolo.—Black, slightly flushed with pink, and spotted with grey and olive green. *Egypt.*

Gr. turchino. B.—Bluish grey with stains of white and spots of shining black. *S. Giov. Port. Lat.*

Gr. violetto. B.—White and violet with small spots of black. *S. Prassede.*

GR. NERO.

Lapis Hethiopicus, from Ethiopia. Black faintly mottled with greenish red. Metallic, spotted with brown rust, like bits of red granite.

S. Cecilia; S. Giov. Lat.—Albani; Egypt.; Octagon; Sciarra.

Gr. nero tigrato.—Black, with large white spots, and tinge of pink.

S. Prassede.—B. N.; Cap.; Egypt.

Gr. nero brecciato. B.—Black, mottled with greenish red, and veined or waved with bright red. Pinkish grey, with fragments of black.

Cap.; Egypt.

Gr. nero rossastro minuto.—Minute dusky grey, tinged with pink and green. *Egypt.*

Gr. nero macchiato.—Black with round grey spots and stains. *S. Cecilia.*

* **Gr. nero verdastro.**—Black, dusted with metallic green. *Octagon.*

GR. BIANCO E NERO.

White, with round and oval black spots evenly distributed (Sienite B.).

S. Giov. Lat.; S. Prassede; S. Saba.—Valentini.

Gr. bianco e nero della Colonna.—Light grey and white, with large oblong black stains, due to crystals of doubtful hornblende, unevenly distributed. B. *S. Prassede; S. N. Tolentino.*

GR. VERDE.

Gr. verde bronzato. B.—Two shades of mottled green on grey metallic ground, spotted with lumps of silver crystal. *Cand.*

Gr. verde confuso. B.—Grey, sprinkled with confused spots of blackish green. *Ara Coeli.*

Gr. verde ad Erbetta. B.—Green, like foliage of grass, on darkish ground. *S. Giov. Lat.—Albani.*

Gr. verde minuto.—Tiny mixture of green, white, and black (diorite B.). *Borghese.*

Gr. verde nereggiante. B.—Blackish green, marbled with spots of green and white. *Kirch. Mus.*

Gr. verde plasmato.—Reddish grey, and green spotted with black. *Animali.*

Gr. verde tigrato.—Finely mottled grey and white, with streaks of gold, and a suspicion of green. *S. Lor. fuori.*

GR. DELLA SEDIA.

White and green, irregularly distributed, with large patches of brownish green (diorite B.).

S. Dionigi ; S. M. Cosm.; S. M. Maggiore ; S. Martino ; S. Pietro.—Mus. Arch.

Gr. minuto della Sedia.—Brownish green entirely absent. *S. Lor. fuori.*

GR. GRAFICO.

LAPIS JUDAICUS.—It is not certain that this granite was known to the Romans, and it is now obtained from quarries in the Tyrol and Siberia.

Earthy grey with black crystal lines like Hebrew letters, and sparkling chips of bronzed mica. *Cand.*

Gr. di Elba.—Greyish white, dotted and punctured with black mica. *Cap.*

Gr. bigio del Sempione.— From quarries near Baveno.

Bluish white freckled with black, and regularly marked with crystals of transparent bluish grey.

S. Antonio di Padova ; S. Paolo.

Gr. rossastro del Sempione.— Feldspar bright pink.

S. Paolo.—Borghese ; Porta del Popolo ; V. Torlonia.

XIV. BASALT.

LAPIS BASANITES.—From Ethiopia (see p. 34).

Basalte bronzino. B. — Bronze, with scarcely visible points of yellow.

S. Giov. Fonte.—Cand. ; Egypt.

B. bruno.— Brownish, very metallic, and faintly spotted with various shades of brown.

S. Croce.—*Doria : B. N.; Busts; Torlonia Corso.*

B. nero.—Black, slightly but closely peppered with grey. *Albani; Egypt.*

B. bigio.—Light grey speckled with bluish grey. *Cap.*

B. bigio macchiato.— Hard close-grained grey, with streaks and patches of lighter hue. *Lat. Mus.* [Everybody calls this *Basalt*, but it much more nearly resembles *Bigio morato* or *Nero antico*.]

B. verde.—Dark green pricked with minute spots of yellowish green.

S. Giov. Fonte.—*Albani; Borghese; Cand.; Cap.; Egypt.; Garden; Octagon.*

PIETRA DI PARAGONE.

LAPIS LYDIUS.—An extremely hard variety of basalt, said to come from Lydia, and to be the touchstone of Metallurgists. The term *Paragone* has however been loosely applied to several very black columns, such as those at a Tomb in the Winter Choir of St. John Lateran, and some others in the Cathedral of Ravenna. The latter almost certainly came from quarries in Dalmatia, which yield a jet black marble called *Nero di Trieste*, having little or no suspicion of white (see *Nero antico*); and to this species I believe the following examples are to be referred.

Jet ebony black with faint streak of mottled white. *Borghese; Egypt.*

XV. TRAVERTINE AND VOLCANIC STONES.

TRAVERTINE.

Lapis Tiburtinus.—A calcareous substance deposited by the *Anio* at Tivoli, and the *Aquae Albulae* at Solfatara (*Handbook*, Rte. 43).

Travertino di Tivoli.—Yellowish white, minutely porous. Sometimes, however, the grain is very compact, as in the first example here given.

S. Luigi ; S. Pietro.—*Colosseum ; Theatre of Marcellus.*

T. del Monte Aventino.—Pale tawny ground, with a look of petrified silkworms.

Steps above the *Piazza di Spagna.*

SELCE.

Lapis Tusculanus.—A basaltic lava produced from the extinct volcano by which was formed the ancient *Lake Regillus*, near Colonna. Dark grey, with white or yellowish crystals (see p. 35).

The Romans used it for paving their roads, and a singularly well-preserved example, both of the material and the careful adjustment of its blocks, may be seen in front of the Temple of Saturn in the Forum (Rte. 6).

MANZIANA.

LAPIS ANITIANUS.—Composed of feldspar and mica, and presenting the appearance of a granite rock which has undergone the action of fire—for which reason it is sometimes called *Lava granitica*. Corsi says that all the fire-hearths in Rome are made of it.

PEPERINO.

LAPIS ALBANUS.—A confused mass of ashes, gravel, and volcanic stones, closely welded together. Quarries near the gate of Albano and the Castle of Marino. Used for stairs and fountain basins, because it grows more consistent by being wetted. It suffers both from frost and heat, and is only found in really good preservation under ground.

Dark greenish grey, studded with black fragments like peppercorns, whence its name.

S. And. (Via Flaminia).—*Belvedere ; Papa Giulio.*

SPERONE.

LAPIS GABINUS.—A variety of Peperino, but harder and more durable, quarried near Castiglione (Rte. 46).

Cloaca Maxima; Tabularium; Ruins of Tusculum.

Both these stones are employed in the ancient wall of the Forum of Augustus (*Handbook to Rome*, Rte. 7), where their colour and weather-resisting qualities may be compared. The upper part is of *Peperino*, and has crumbled away at the corners, while the lower courses, in *Sperone*, have their edges as sharp as ever.

TUFO.

LAPIS RUBER.—A conglomerate of ashes and sand thrown out of the crater of a volcano. It is abundant all over the country between Rome and the extinct volcanoes of Latium, and was the earliest building material used in the construction of the city and its walls.

Tufo lionato. B.—Tawny grey, with suspicion of black mica. *Sepolcro dei Nasoni.*

Tufo rosso.—Tawny red, with spots of white, ash, and black. Peppered with shiny mica.

Walls of Servius Tullius; Tarpeian Rock; S. M. Sole; S. M. Egiziaca; S. N. Cesarini.

PART III.

LIST OF CHURCHES AND OTHER BUILDINGS IN WHICH THE PRINCIPAL MARBLES ARE FOUND.

All places are arranged in strictly alphabetical order.

INDEX FOR READY REFERENCE TO HEADINGS.

Arches, 147.
Campidoglio, 147.
Campo Santo, 147.
Chiesa Nuova, 147.
Churches, 148.
Cloaca Maxima, 186.
Collegio Romano, 186.
Colosseum, 186.
Forum, 186.
Fountain, 186.
Hospital, 186.
Lateran, 187.
Museums, 187.
Obelisks, 189.
Oratory, 186.
Palazzo, 189.
Pantheon, 186.

Piazza, 192.
Pincio, 192.
Porta, 192.
Porticus, 192.
Pyramid, 192.
Sacristy, 178.
Scala Santa, 186.
Scuola, 192.
Sepolcro, 192.
Suffragio (S. M. del), 185.
Tarpeian Rock, 192.
Temple, 187.
Theatre, 192.
University, 192.
Vatican, 192.
Via, 199.
Villa, 199.

TECHNICAL ITALIAN NAMES.

Balustri, short pillars of an altar railing.
Cancello, altar railing.
Facciata, front of a building.
Fascia, band or fillet.
Gradino, shelf at the back of an altar.
Lastra, slab.
Lastrina, little slab.
Paliotto, front of an altar.
Pilastrini, short pilasters in a Cancello.
Rocchio, stump of a column.
Sfondi, recesses between the side of an altar and any neighbouring projection.
Specchio (mirror), vertical slab of marble in a frame or moulding at the foot of a column.
Stela, short upright gravestone.
Tazza, shallow bowl, usually round, but sometimes square.
Zoccolo, plinth.

ABBREVIATIONS.

N.B.—*Genera* begin with capitals; *species* with small letters.

Affr. *Affricano.*
Al. *Alabastro.*
B. *Francesco Belli.*
Br. *Breccia.*
br. *brecciato-a.*
C. *Corsi.*
Cip. *Cipollino.*
col *Column.*
Cor. *Corallina.*
cor. *corallino-a.*
dend. *dendritico-a.*
dor. *dorato-a.*
erbor. *erborizzato.*
F. di Persico, *Fiore di Persico.*
fior. *fiorito-a.*
fort. *fortezzino.*
gatt. *gatteggiante.*
Gr. *Granito.*
inter. *interrupted* (as to the fluting).
H. W. *Holy Water Basin.*
list. *listato-a.*
Lum. *Lumachella.*
lum. *lumachellato-a.*
mand. *mandolato.*
min. *minuto-a.*
mor. *morato.*
nuv. *nuvolato-a.*
Occhio di Pav. *Occhio di Pavone.*
Occhio di Pav. pav. *Occhio di Pavone pavonazzo.*
pall. *pallido-a.*
ond. *ondato-a.*
Pav. *Pavonazzetto.*
pav. *pavonazzo-a.*
Porf. *Porfido.*

P. santa, *Porta santa.*
R. *Ravestein.*
ran. *ranocchia.*
S. *Sapienza* (University).
Sard. (sard.) *Sardonico.*
Serp. *Serpentina.*

serp. *serpentino.*
Trac. *Traccagnina.*
ven. *venato-a.*
trans. transept.
turc. *turchiniccio.*

Arch of Constantine.—Seven fluted cols *Giallo antico dor.* Col nearest Meta Sudans, *Carrara.*
Seven Dacian prisoners, *Pav.;* 3rd from the left, on side towards S. Gregorio, new.
Arch of Drusus.—Two cols *Giallo antico.*
Arch of Janus.—*Imezio.*
Arch of Sept. Severus.—Eight fluted cols *Imezio* (inside).
Arch of Titus, *Pentelico.*—Two cols outside, partly buried, *Imezio.*
Campidoglio.—Castor and Pollux, *Pentelico.* Milestones, *Carrara antico* and *Cip.*
Catacombs of St. Alexander.—At entrance to Basilica, two cols *Gr. persichino.*

CHURCHES.

(In strictly alphabetical order.)

Campo Santo.—Two fluted cols *Carrara macchiato* in chapel on the rt.
Chiesa Nuova.
1st rt., four slabs above arches of doors, *Lum. gialla;* eight narrow, oblong slabs, *Settebasi pav.* S.
2nd rt., four pilasters on walls, *Cip. rosso diasprato* B (*ond.* R); two cols *Br. di Simone;* two large slabs beneath, *Lum. bigia bruna.*
3rd rt., hexagons on pavement, *Palombino bianco* B; two cols *Giallo dor. cupo.*

4th rt., on cancello, *Pav. verdiccio* B; on walls, *Br. bruna* R (*marrone*); two cols *Al. bruno rossastro*.
5th rt., on cancello, **Br. pav. min.*
6th rt., two cols *Verde antico*.
Pilaster on rt. at gate in cancello, *F. di Persico reticolare*.
Chapel to rt. of tribune, fascia of pedestals within cancello, *Settebasi bigia rossastra*; outside cancello, *Br. Gregoriana*.
High altar, four cols *P. santa gialla rossastra*.
Tomb on left, two cols *Bianco e nero antico*; on rt., two of *Bianco e nero di Francia*.
7th left, four cols *Al. giallastro unv.*
6th left, two cols *Verde antico*.
5th left, two fluted cols *Pav. bianco*; four specchi on cancello, *Affr. cor. piritifero* B (*bigio piritifero* R).
4th left, two cols *Astracane maschio* (*bruno*); over doors, squares of *Cor. scura*; outside pilasters, *P. Santa bigia orbicolare* B.
3rd left, two cols *Giallo antico*.
2nd left, four pilasters on cancello, *Br. rosca* B (*Trac. rossastra*); walls of *P. Santa rossastra conchigliare* S.

Church of the Agonizzanti.

2nd rt., two cols *P. santa bruna e rossastra*; opposite, four specchi of *Pecorella a rosa*.

Annunziata.—Paliotto of three altars, *Al. giallo list.* S.
Beata Rita.—Under organ, col on l., *Pav. dor.*; rt., *Br. pav*.
Divina Pietà.—Two H. W. of *P. santa*; six lastre on Cancello *Cor. di Cori*.
Divino Amore.—On the rt., gradino and paliotto of **Cip. verde* (*chiaro*); gradino of high altar, *Affr. sanguigno*.
Gesù.—Two large cols at main door, *Serravezza fior.*; spheres on all lateral cancelli, **Cottanello antico*; oblongs of *Diaspro tenero*.
2nd rt., two cols *Porf. rosso*.
3rd rt., two cols *Verde antico*; slab on pedestal in each corner, *Al. rosso* B.
Two slabs at entrance, *Al. marino* S; eight octagons of *Spato fluore*.

5th rt., at entrance, two cols *Affr. cor.*; two cols on the rt., *Cor. pall.* B; two on the l., *Cor. rosea* R.

Tomb on pavement in front of Chapel, *Lum. nera di Etiopia* S; small bits at corners of slabs under arch, *Al. eburneo* B.

High altar, cancello, *Cip. mand. verde* B. Doors within the tribune, four pilasters of **Al. orientale fort. lum.* B; inner jambs, *F. di Persico reticolare*; four cols *Giallo antico*; paliotto, *Spato fluore*; lower plinth of cols *Cip. marino* B; pilasters on walls *Settebasi gialla* B; gradino **Lum. gialla e pav.* S; plinths below, *Br. dor.*, and *Br. verde di Egitto*; steps of *Gr. tigrato*.

5th left, Cancello, *Diaspro (Al.) a rosa cinabrino*: two cols *Affr.*; two *P. santa*; two *Cor. ven.*

4th left, four large oblongs on walls, *Al. orientale occhiuto* B; on pavement, *Verde chiaro* S; sphere covered with *Lapis lazzuli* B.

3rd left, two cols *Cor. pall*; two slabs at entrance, *Br. policroma trac. rossastra* S.

1st left, 5th left, and Sacristy, two cols *Giallo antico*.

Gesù e Maria.

2nd l., 2 cols *Br. pav.*; frieze of cancello, *Lum. rosea* B; paliotto, *Al. onichino*; gradino, *Al. giallo list.* S.

1st left, two fluted cols *Bardiglio*. 4th l., urn of *Calcarea bigia*.

Priorato.—Plinth of 2nd tomb on the left, *Bigio ven.*

[**Regina Coeli.**—At tomb near high altar, two cols of **Nero antico*. Stem of H. W., *F. di Persico*.]

S. Adriano.—Two large cols at high altar, *Porf. rosso*.

1st left, two cols *Bianco e nero di Francia*; four small slabs on walls, *Br. trac.* S. 3rd l., on paliotto, two oblongs of *Br. pav. confuso.*

S. Agata dei Goti. —Twelve unique cols of **Gr. bruno giallastro*. On gradino, four oblongs of **Semesantone bigio*. On altar, *V. ran. orbicolare.*

S. Agata in Trastevere.—Cancello of *P. santa br. lum.*

S. Agnese fuori le Mura.—*Four cols *P. santa*, the largest in Rome; last col but one on the rt., *P. santa fior.* B; last col on the rt., *P. santa lionata ramificata* R.

Eight cols *Pav. br.*; *two fluted and moulded *Pav.*; 1st and 2nd col rt. *Pav. bruno* B (*scuro angoloso* R).
Cols of baldacchino, *Porf. rosso lattinato* B (*cioccolato* S); statue of Saint, *Al. verdognolo.*

S. Agnese in Piazza Navona.—Four inter. cols *Verde antico*.
In sacristy, two small cols *Verde scuro*.

S. Agostino. —2nd rt., two cols *Broccatellone*.
5th rt., two long pilasters *Br. fruttieolosa min.*
7th rt., two cols *Affr.*
Tombs under cupola against pier rt. and left *Br. di Aleppo*; on the left, candelabrum of *Bigio antico*; fillet, *Lum. nera min.*
7th left, two cols *Giallo carnagione*.
1st left, two cols *Portasanta tigrata*.
Refectory, six cols *Tasio*.

S. Alessio.—Tomb to rt. of entrance, specchi of *Sard. bianco.
3rd rt., two cols *Broccatellone*; fascia on tabernacle, *Semesanto giallo*; gradino, *Bianco e nero di Perugia*.
High altar, four cols *Verde antico*; specchi, *Occhio di Pav. rosso*; plinth, *Affr. verde*.
Crypt, six cols *Gr. del Foro*.

S. Ambrogio.
1st rt., two fluted cols *Taormina*.
2nd, two cols *Al. bruno*.
3rd, two *Porto Venere*.
3rd l., two *Serravezza pall.*; below them, four ridged octagons of *Br. fruttieolosa min.*
2nd, strips on paliotto, *Affr. sanguigno confuso*; two small cols *P. santa violacea*.
1st, two cols *Bianco e nero di Porto Ferrajo*; on paliotto, leaves of *Verde di Firenze* S (many picked out).

S. Anastasia.
Nave, four cols at the corners, *Gr. di Giglio*; one fluted *Imezio*; one (to l. of door), *Bigio alabastrino*; seven *Pav.*; two (large) *P. Santa*.
1st rt., two half cols *P. santa carnagione*.
two cols *Rosso di Francia*.

Rt. trans., gradino of *Br. bianca e nera* S.
1st left, two spiral cols *Pav.*
Left trans., two cols *Al. giallo br.;* sides of altar, *Settebasi gatt.*

S. Andrea delle Fratte.
2nd rt. and *3rd left, two cols *P. Santa.* Below the latter, oblongs of *Plasma di Smeraldo.* Gradino *Br. verde di Egitto.*

S. Andrea al Quirinale.
Side walls at high altar, *Bigio br. min. schietto* S; four cols of *Cottanello rosso scuro* R.
Fillet of paliotto in Cappella Stanislao, *Rosso br. bruno* B.

S. Andrea in Via Flaminia.
Corinthian front of *Peperino.*

S. Andrea in Vincis.
High altar, two cols *P. Santa.*

S. Andrea della Valle.
1st rt., four cols *Verde antico*, and two at tomb on rt.; [two outside cols at altar, *Verde antico ond.* B]; under cols at altar, *Cotognino dend.;* paliotto of *Plasma di Smeraldo* C; corner pilasters, *Al. a rosa list.;* below, *Bigio e nero minuto.* Band on pavement under arch, *P. santa violacea poligonia* B.
2nd rt., pedestals of outside arch, *Broccatello melleo*, B; four pedestals of lateral arches, *P. Santa fior.* B; two slabs under bronze statues, *Al. fior. muscoso* B; oblongs behind the four urns, *Al. a rosa list.;* plinth below urn (Lor. Strozzi), *Br. dor. orbicolare* B; twelve inter. cols and half cols, *Lum. violetta* (*lionata* R); twelve small slabs of *Giallo focato.*
Cancello of high altar, mixture of *Astracanc giallo* (femina) and *A. verdastro* (maschio) B; [mixture of *A. dorato* and *A. bruno* R]; many slabs of *Diaspro rosso e giallo list.;* below candelabra, *Trac. min.*
2nd left, outside the chapel, two small squares of *Giallo tigrato* B; fascia all round the chapel, *Br. marrone* S; above it, four oblongs, *Al. marino* S; above these, on pilasters at entrance, *Afr. cor. zonale* B; at corners, eight small squares of *Br. Quintilina* R; between them, four small oblongs of *Al. a rosa*

sfrangiato B ; above, eight long vertical strips of *Giallo br. dor.* R ; two small ovals on gradino, *Sard. tartarugato scuro ;* two cols *Porto Venere ;* two cols *Broccatellone ;* narrow oblongs below four cols, *Al. giallognolo ;* two half cols at each door, *Lum. bigia.*

1st left, many slabs of *Verde di Susa ;* two small oblongs beside altar, *Tartaruga list.* S.

S. Angelo in Pescheria.
2nd rt., two cols *Affr. pav.*
Specchi of *Rosso brecciato*, with narrow pebbles; cancello, *Bigio conchigliare.*
On the front of the church, three fluted cols *Pentelico.*

SS. Angeli Custodi.
Altar rt., two half cols *Cip. bigio.*
High altar, large fillet of *Lum. bigia di Egitto* S.

S. Antonio ai Monti.
Four cols *Pav.* at porch.

S. Antonio degli Armeni.
High altar, two *chased cols *Pentelico.*

S. Antonio di Padova.—Cols of *Gr. bigio del Sempione.*

S. Antonio dei Portoghesi.
3rd rt., doors of *Cor. grigia pall. min.* S.
Pilasters of *Diaspro tenero conchigliare.*
Rt. trans. Zoccoli of urn, *Bigio e nero min.*
Left trans. *Urn beneath altar, *Bigio br. min.* S (*Greco mand.* B).
Two urns over doors, *Bianco e nero tigrato* B.
2nd left, two cols *F. di Persico.*

S. Apollinare.—Tassels of arms at tomb on pavement of atrium, *Verde di Firenze* S.
Zoccoli of outside pilasters in Chancel, *Affr. nero br.* S.
2nd left, background of Crucifix, *Bigio (fort.* S) *alabastrino* B.

SS. Apostoli.—Chapel at end of rt. aisle, eight large fluted cols *Lesbio* C.
High altar, two slabs at each end on cancello, *Broccatello principe* S. Two cols at tomb on rt. wall of chancel, *Br. verde di Egitto scura.*

S. Balbina.
Mouldings of altar surrounding urn, *P. santa br. min.*
S. Bartolommeo.
Specchi below cols at end of rt. aisle, *Bigio scuro macchiato.*
High altar, urn of *Porf. rosso* ; plinth, *Bigio list.;* steps of *Pav. verde.*
S. Benedetto.—Chapel on left, col of *Cotognino* and of *Tasio* C.
S. Bernardino.
1st left, two cols *Giallo melleo* B ; above the altar *Occhio di Pav. verdognolo* B; gradino, *Affr. nero ;* plinth, *Greco scritto confuso.*
S. Bernardo.
Pilasters of tomb on rt., and specchi below cols on left, *Settebasi dor.* R.
Altar, rt. and left, two cols *Verde chiaro.*
Cancello, rt. and left, **Trac. policroma minuto.* Cancello to rt., four tiny scraps of *Lum. pav.* on the top.
High altar, lower gradino, *Br. pav. reticolata ;* paliotto and upper gradino, *Palombara bianco list.*
S. Bibiana.
In the nave, two spirally fluted cols *Lesbio.*
High altar, urn of *Al. bianco.*
1st left, two cols ** Cor. violacea.* Square col to l. of door, *Rosso antico.*
S. Brigida.
Panels on paliotto of all three altars, *Verde cip.* B ; narrow plinth, below cancello of high altar, *Settebasi gatt.*
S. Calisto.—Cancello of **Sard. tartarugato agatino* B ; other specchi of *Broccatello giallo* and *violacco*, showing contrast.
At high altar, two *pilasters of *Affr. verde.*
S. Carlo al Corso.
On walls in rt. transept, *four slabs of *Cip. marino.*
S. Carlo ai Catinari.
1st rt., large slab on altar, *Al. orientale occhiuto* B ; four slabs on cancello, *F. di Persico giallastro* R.
2nd rt., two cols *P. santa ;* on paliotto *Al. fort.* S.
Last rt., two small tapering fluted cols **Settebasi bigia* C.
High altar, on gradino, **Palombara brunastro.* S; four cols *Porf. rosso.*

Sacristy, two cols *Br. rossa.*
3rd left, on gradino, *Settebasi dor.* ; jambs of doors, *Lum. rossa* B.
2nd left, on pedestal of cols, *Al. onichino ;* sfondi, *P. santa bigia fior.*
Fillet at 1st left, and zoccoli of cols 2nd left, *Br. trac.* S.
1st left, paliotto, *F. di Persico confuso ;* two cols *Verde antico ;* H. W. on left, **Br. gialla e nera* C.

S. Catarina.
1st rt., pilasters of *Sard. orientale list.* S. ; side walls and picture frame, *P. santa rossastra br. scura ;* below cols, and tablet below picture, *Al. a rosa list.*
1st rt., lower walls, 1st left, lower pilasters, *Settebasi gutt.* B.
2nd rt., below cols *Tartaruga fior.* S.
High altar, fillet of *Br. pav. trac.* B.
3rd left, on pavement, two lozenges of *Br. trac. violetta* (*Br. frutticolosa*) ; on lower pilasters, ovals of *Al. bigio dor.* within border of *Broccatellone pav. ;* on specchi, lozenges of *Al. fior. list.* S ; on gradino, *Br. Quintilina ;* on paliotto, **Al. pav. occhiuto* and *Lapis lazzuli macchiato.*
2nd left, below picture, *Palombara tartarugato* B ; on side walls, four slabs of *Al. melleo list.*
1st left, paliotto of *Al. verdognolo list. ;* below picture, *Al. onichino ;* below cols, *Al. giallo list.* S.

S. Catarina dei Funari.
2nd rt., two cols *Giallo br.*
3rd rt., two cols *Bigio antico,* inclining to *Affr.*
High altar, on cancello, *Giallo pall.* S ; two cols *Verde di Susa.*
Last left, on cancello, two balls of *Br. pav. sfrangiata* B.
1st left, two cols *Verde di Ponsevera chiaro ;* specchi and upper gradino, *Tartaruga list. ;* on cancello, four pilastrini of *Broccatello melleo.*

S. Catarina da Siena.
Pilasters of *Giallo e nero di Siena ;* four minor altars framed in *Imezio fasciato schietto.*

S. Cecilia.
Portico, cols of *Affr.,* partly *A. rosso br.,* partly *A. nero ond.* B.
1st rt., on paliotto, two circles of **Rosso lum.* Two cols *Bigio scritto :* in bathroom, two of *Gr. nero macchiato.*

Tomb. of Card. Sfondrati, specchio of *Pecorella min. nuv.* B; another of *Al. a rosa nuv. dor.* R; lowest plinth, *Affr. giallognolo* B; sfondi of *Br. trac.* S; 2nd rt., col on rt., *Bigio lum. piccolo* R.
At door on rt., two large spiral cols *Tasio*; jambs of door, *Giallo focato* B.
5th rt., two cols *P. santa.*
High altar, frieze of cornice at cancello, *Broccatello giallo* R.
Two oval slabs inside cancello, beside statue of Saint, *Al. a rosa corniolino*; two slabs on outer pavement, and two beside statue, *Al. marino* S; pavement in front of statue, *Al. fiorito mellco* B.
Four cols of baldacchino, *Bianco e nero antico.
2nd left, two cols *Bigio chiaro* S; urn at 2nd tomb left *Cip. bigio rigato.*
1st left, two cols *Gr. nero.*

S. Cesareo.
Altar, rt. and left, two cols *Pav.*, and two strips of damaged *Cip. rosso.*
Round slab on pulpit, *Porf. serp. verde agatato* B.
High altar, four cols *Broccatellone*: many good varieties of *Porf. rosso* and *Porf. serp. verde* on screen.

S. Claudio.
Paliotto of high altar, *Cotognino arancio.*

S. Clemente.
1st rt., fillet under cols, *Settebasi policroma* S.
End of left aisle, two cols *Br. pav. trac.*
In nave, four fluted cols *Imezio.*
Baldacchino, *two cols *Pav. br. min.* and *two *Bigio scritto*, placed diagonally; small bits on pavement near rt. ambo, *Al. orientale pomellato* B.
LOWER CHURCH.—Rt. aisle, near entrance on the left, buried col of *Verde principe*; other cols of *Bigio*, *P. Santa*, *Nero*, *Bigio chiaro*, granite and *Cip.*, all half buried.
Baldacchino cols *Serravezza nobile.*

SS. Cosma e Damiano.
Outside, facing the Forum, col on rt., *Porf. rosso pomato.*

Between rotunda and nave, two half-buried spheres of *Nefritica verde*.
1st rt., two cols *Broccatello sanguigno* B (*Lum. pav.* C).
High altar, four cols *Bianco e nero di Francia*.
SS. Cosma e Damiano (in Trastevere).
At gateway, col of *Pario* C. In the court, large sculptured bath of *Gr. del Foro*.
Two door-jambs and smaller hatch, *Bigio br. chiaro*.
S. Costanza.
Two cols *Gr. del Foro*; four *Gr. rosso*; 18 *Gr. persichino*.
On paliotto, four small bits of *Br. dor. min.*
S. Crisogono.
Tomb near principal door, urn of *Calcarea bigia*.
Several cols in nave, *Gr. rosco fasciato* B; 8th col rt., *Gr. rosso macchiato* B.
Two large cols *Porf. rosso confuso* R; cols of baldacchino, *Al. di Montauto*.
Chapel on left, paliotto of *Rosso di Levanto*; cancello, *Giallo carnagione disfatto*.
Stem of H. W. on left, *Affr. verde lum.* B.
S. Croce.
Portico, on l., col *Bardiglio list.* R; patched with *Bigio lum.*
1st col rt., *Gr. rosso pall.* Cancello on rt., fine plinth of *Pav. nero*.
2nd rt. and left, two tiny squares, *Br. gialla rossastra* S, and two of *Al. onichino*.
3rd rt. and left, at foot of paliotto, *Rosso br. min.* B (*scuro*).
Urn at high altar, *Basalte bruno*; leaves of tomb on pavement in front, *Verde di Firenze* S; two cols at baldacchino, *Cor. pav. scura* R; two, *P. santa bicolore*.
3rd l., on paliotto, two slabs of *Al. violetto list.*
1st and 2nd cols on left in nave, *Gr. del Giglio* C.
S. Croce dei Lucchesi.
1st rt., round the urn, *F. di Persico picchiettato*; outside pilasters, two vertical strips of *Affr. bigio ven.*; gradino, *Al. rosso e giallo list.*

S. Dionigi.
At high altar, two cols *Taormina*; plinth under tabernacle, *Gr. della Sedia*. Gradino of *P. Santa*.

SS. Domenico e Sisto.
1st rt., two cols *Diaspro tenero*; pilasters behind them, *Diaspro conchigliare*; plinth of *Settebasi gatt.* S; gradino, *Al. fort.* S.

3rd rt., plinth of *Br. trac.* S; gradino of *Al. fior. list.*

High altar, paliotto of *Al. bianco a nuvole* S; on walls, large and small slabs of *Br. Quintilina* B; slabs above small arches, *Br. pav. reticolata* S; two pilastrini of cancello, *Giallo br. pall.*; two of *Sard. macchiato* S.

3rd left, two ovals on side walls, *Sard. tartarugato scuro.*

2nd left, picture framed in *Bianco e nero di Perugia.*

1st left, ground of cross on paliotto, *Bigio perlato* B; on gradino, *Al. fior. list.*; two long vertical slips, *Cor. scura.*

S. Dorotea.
2nd rt., and l. on altar, *Al. melleo cupo* B (*Al. di Montauto giallastro*).

Upper and lower mouldings of both altars, *Lum. pav.* B.

1st left, paliotto of *P. santa violocea poligonia* B.

S. Eligio dei Ferrai.
High altar, two cols *Al. di Civitavecchia*; on gradino, *Al. a rosa* and *Al. onichino.*

2nd l., below cols, *Rosso br.*

1st l., on gradino, *F. di Persico chiaro.*

S. Eusebio.—High altar, two outside cols, *Cor. pav.*; two inside, *Broccatellone.* Specchi below outer cols, *Br. dor.*; gradino of side altars, *Br. pav.*

S. Eustachio.—2nd rt., two cols *P. santa bruna bicolore.*

High altar, urn of *Porf. rosso*; gradino, *Br. trac. lum.* S; lower plinth, *Settebasi mand.* S.

1st left, moulded gradino of *F. di Persico rosso.*

[S. Faustino.
High altar, col on left, *Giallo br. dor.*; on rt., *Giallo fasciato*; cancello, *P. santa lum.*]

S. Francesca Romana.
Tomb on rt., two cols *Giallo alabastrino*.
Top of cancello, **Bigio macchiato scuro*.

S. Francesco di Paola.
At tomb on the rt., two half cols *Tasio*, two *Affr.*

S. Francesco a Ripa.
3rd rt., two cols *Giallo antico*.
5th rt., two cols *Affr. nero*.
High altar, lower gradino of *Pav. br. dorato*, upper, *Palombara dend*. S.
Gradino of two side altars, *Br. pav.* S.
5th left, two cols *P. santa*.

S. Giacomo a Scossa-cavalli.
1st left, on paliotto, *P. santa rossastra*.

S. Giacomo al Corso.
2nd rt., frame of altar-piece and two large pilasters, *Br. pav. lineare* S.
3rd rt., two cols *Verde antico*; two slabs on gradino, *Br. verde* S.
High altar, *four cols *Affr. bigio*; plinths below them, *Al. fior. spezzato* B.
At tabernacle, twelve colonnettes, *Verde pall.*
3rd left, two cols *Bigio mor.*; gradino, *Pecorella sanguigno*.
2nd left, gradino, *Palombara violetto*.

S. Giacomo degli Spagnuoli.
Two cols *P. santa*, partly buried.
Chapel on rt., fluted pilasters of *Carrara*; cancello of *Imezio*.

S. Gioacchino.—Sides of altar to rt., *Cip. ondato*.

S. Giorgio.
In portico, two cols *Lesbio* B; 1st on rt., *Gr. bigio terrco* B.
In the nave, two fluted *Tasio*, two fluted *Pav.*; 6th col on the left, *Gr. persichino*.

S. Giovanni Decollato.—High altar, two cols *Verde antico*.

S. Giovanni dei Fiorentini.
1st rt., two cols *Affr. bigio*.
2nd rt., two cols *Broccatellone*.

3rd rt., two cols *P. sauta*.
4th rt., under picture, *Bigio list*.
6th rt., two cols *Bianco c ncro di Fraucia*.
Tomb at last pilaster rt., *Scmcsanto giallo*.
High altar, cols of *Cottaucllo dor*. R; base of tomb at 5th pilaster left, *F. di Persico sanguiguo* B.
Upper plinth, end of left aisle, *Cor. pall. nuv.* S.
4th left, two cols *P. sauta*.
3rd left, two cols *Giallo br.*; on the wall behind urns, *P. sauta lionata* B.
2nd left, slab on each side wall, *Lum. rossa* S.
1st left, two cols *Settebasi grigia* B (*min.*).

S. Giovanni in Fonte.
Two cols *Porf. rosso coufuso* (largest in Rome); eight cols *Porf. rosso scuro plasmato*.
Font of *Basalte verde* C (*bronzino* B); slabs on pavement *Affr. bigio ven.*; two slabs at corners in upper pavement, *Giallo a nuvole* S.
1st rt., two small spiral cols **Porf. serp. verde cupo* R; capitals and bases, *Porf. serp. verde* B.
Chapel on rt., two cols *Porf. rosso* C.
Altar of SS. Cyprian and Justina, **Settebasi ven.* S.
1st left, col on rt., *Al. perlaceo* B; on left, *Al. bianco* C.
Altar on left, *Serp. br. ncra* R.

S. Giovanni dei Genovesi.
—High altar, two cols *Porf. pav.*; on paliotto, eight squares **Al. dor.*; two pieces of *Br. pav. miu*.

S. Giovanni in Laterano.
Door-jambs of Porta Santa, *P. s. bigia orbicolare* B.
In nave, twenty-four cols *Verde mand.* R.
Four pilasters of side door, *Cip. rosso fasciato* B (horribly splayed).
Rt. trans., two large fluted cols *Giallo autico*; base, *Affr. rosso dor. dend.* R (*A. rosso crbor.* B).
Behind Choir, pilaster of Tomb (Card. Filippucci), *Settebasi violacca* B.
Tomb of Card. Muti Papazzurri, *Gr. nero* with small bits of *Gr. tigrato bianco* B.

1st Sacristy, two pilastrini at further end, *P. santa rossastra br. scura* S; two cols **Gr. bianco e nero*; two cols **Gr. bigio*.
2nd Sacristy, two cols *Taormina*.
Left trans. col on rt., *Giallo carnagione* B; l., *Giallo nuv.*; four cols at altar, *Verde antico* C; fillets of Cancello, *Settebasi dor*.
WINTER CHOIR (closed with glass door).
 Piers of arch outside entrance, *Cor. lum.* B; inside, *Cor. giallognola* B.
 Two cols **Nero antico* C; four of **Al. brunastro fiorito*.
CLOISTER.—Col of *Cor. pall.*; six cols *Pav.* C; two engrailed half cols of *Pentelico*.
LEFT AISLE.—3rd chapel, two cols *P. santa pall.* Tomb nearly opposite, two cols *Giallo antico*.
2nd left, slab on pavement under gate, *Br. gialla rossastra* S.
CAPP. DI S. ANDREA CORSINI.
 Four cols and urn of *Porf. rosso*; oblongs in sfondi, *Al. rosso e giallo* S; pavement, *Serp. reticolata dell' Elba* S.
 Oblong on pavement in nave, nearly opposite the Chapel, **Gr. verde ad erbetta* B.
CAPPELLA TORLONIA.—On cancello, *Cip. mand. grande*; pilasters, *Giallo pallido* and *G. br.* (both spoilt by splaying); on walls, *Trac. bruna dor.*

S. Giovanni e Paolo.

Two cols, inside doorway, **Greco dislocato*.
Slab at memorial stone in the nave, *Pav. bianco ven.*
Candlebearer, **Al. fior. list.* C.
Cancello of high altar, *Verde picchiettato*.
CAPP. TORLONIA.
 On lower gradino, *Cip. mand.*; on upper, choice agates framed in *Semesanto pav.*
 On walls, *Sard. occhiuto chiaro* framed in *Verde di Grecia*; long slab, *Trac. confusa* framed in *Palombara list.* above *V. di Persico*.
 Beside these, handsome splayed slabs of *Cip. rosso*.
 On pavement, five large circles, *Br. di Simone diasprato*.

S. Giovanni della Pigna.

Paliotto of four side altars, *P. santa rossastra br. scura* S.

S. Giovanni a Porta Latina.
In atrium, two cols *Tasio*, two fluted *Pentelico*.
Two cols *Cip. bigio*, two fluted *Pav.*
4th col rt. and left, *Gr. del Foro turc.* B.

S. Girolamo della Carità.
1st left, two small cols *Bigio lum. grande* B.
2nd, two cols *Broccatellone* C.
Rt. trans., tomb tablet, *Astracane femina.*
High altar, four inter. cols *Taormina ;* at corners of arch, four slabs, **Al. tartaruga brunastro.*
Cancello on left, lowest plinth, *Affr. carnino :* upper plinth and pilastrini *P. santa br.*

S. Giuseppe a Capo le Case.
Paliotto of two side altars, *Palombara rossastro.* S.

S. Giuseppe alla Lungara.
1st rt. and l., frame of paliotto, *Occhio di Pav. pav.* S.
Lower step, **Cip. verde ond.*
High altar, frame of *Occhio di Pav. bruno ;* lower gradino, *F. di Persico ven.* ; upper, *Giallo di Siena br.*

S. Gregorio.
ATRIUM.—Two cols *Bigio mor.* ; two *P. santa* ; two *Cor. rossa e gialla.*
1st tomb on left, two pilasters, *Bigio chiaro* S; 6th, two cols *Bigio lum.*
5th tomb on left, two small bits of *Br. gialla rossastra* S.
NAVE.—On pavement near door, small bits of *Gr. bigio min.*
2nd left, paliotto, *Al. fior. giallo* B.
3rd left, front of urn, *Al. a rosa giallo* B.
Large Chapel on left, *two cols *Bigio ven. di giallo* (*Giallo e nero* B); four cols **Cip. verde.*
CAPP. ANDREA.—Two cols *Verde chiaro* (lightest in Rome).
Table on rt., stem of **Pav. cupo.*
CAPP. BARBARA.—*Two cols *Br. rossastra* ; chair of *Cip. rosso.*
CAPP. SILVIA.—Two cols *Porf. rosso* C ; frieze and specchi of **Al. tartaruga brunastro.*
Jambs of niche for Saint, *Giallo bigiastro.*

S. Ignazio.

1st rt., gradino of *Al. fort.*
2nd rt., on cancello, *Giallo br. principe* S.
3rd rt., circle of *Sard. pomato.*
Plinth round choir, *Br. pav. grande.*
Beside cols on wall of left trans., *Cotognino orientale chiaro* B; at corners of large relief, *Al. onichino.*
SACRISTY.—*Two cols *Bianco e nero antico* C. Rich scraps of *Settebasi dor., Br. trac.*, and alabasters.
1st left, on paliotto *Sard. a rosa nuv.*

S. Isidoro.

Cancello, 1st rt. and left, *Settebasi rossa schiacciata.*
2nd rt., on cancello, *Palombara eburneo.*
High altar, strips of *Al. melleo fior. di rosa*; cancello to rt., *Cor. rosea* B (*pall.* R).
Cancello to left, two pilasters *Al. tartaruga pall. occhiuto.*
1st left, *two small inter. cols *Giallo antico.*

S. Lazzaro.

Two cols *Bigio antico*; two *Imezio*; two *Gr. bigio.*
2nd left, two cols *Bigio antico* C.

S. Lorenzo in Borgo.

Eight cols *Bigio lum.* C. Col of *Imezio dentellato.*
3rd col left, *Bigio azzurrognolo* B; 7th left, *Greco scritto* B.
High altar, two cols *Al. a giaccione* B.

S. Lorenzo in Damaso.

Baldacchino cols of *Cotognino orientale.*

S. Lorenzo fuori le Mura.

In portico, four spiral cols *Pav.* C.
In nave, six cols *Cip. verde.*
1st tomb rt., two cols *Tasio* C.
Tomb at end of rt. aisle, plinth of *Lum. bigia*; fine slabs of *Al. melleo list.* and *Cotognino.*
Rt. ambo, large round slab of *Porf. serp. verde cupo* C.
Baldacchino cols *Porf. rosso* C.
High altar, paliotto of *Porf. rosso pomato.*
Chancel cols *Pav. tigrato* R; on pavement, *Porf. pav.* B (*bigio turc.*), and many varieties of granite.

On screen, fourteen slabs in two rows—upper, *Porf. serp. verde;* lower, *Porf. rosso*, in great variety.

6th Square on wall to rt., *Porf. serp. verde bruno* B; round slab at back of chair, *Gr. min. della Sedia* B; *two cols above, *Gr. verde tigrato* C.

In confession, four cols *Verde biancastro min.*; sphere of *Nefritica*.

End of left aisle, *Lum. bigia* R (*nera di Etiopia*); in cloister, col of *Cip. verde*.

S. Lorenzo in Fonte.

Cancello of two chapels, balustri of *Astracane giallo* (*femina*) B; pilastrini of *Affr. sanguigno*.

Gradino on left, *Cor. pav. pall.* and *Cor. rossa scura*.

Tomb on left, two strips of *Br. di Aleppo;* paliotto of high altar, *Al. rosso fort.* B.

S. Lorenzo in Lucina.

Below tomb to rt. of door, *Al. tartaruga rigato.* S.

2nd rt., two sfondi of *Lum. nera min.* S; specchi, *Semesanto pav.* S.

3rd rt., gradino, *Palombara list. fior.* S; *Al. occhiuto* S.

Mouldings of high altar, and paliotto of altar to rt., *Occhio di pernice* B. Cols of *B. e N. di Porto Ferrajo*.

3rd left, pilasters of cancello, *Cor. lionata* S.

S. Lorenzo in Miranda.

Ten large cols, *Cip. verde list.* (*zonale* B).

Fillet below cols at high altar, *Semesanto pav. min.*

S. Lorenzo in Panisperna.

Tabernacle at high altar, eight colonnettes, *Al. ametistino* B (*violetto* R); on cancello, two spheres, *Cor. pav. min.*; 2nd rt., urn of *Bigio br. min.*; 1st rt., two oblongs *Br. frutticolosa*, and two *Br. rossa e gialla min.* on cancello.

S. Luca.—Eight cols *Bardiglio;* eight *Serravezza pav.;* urn of *Sard. scuro* (see *S. Martina*).

S. Lucia dei Ginnasi.

High altar, two cols *P. santa* C.

S. Lucia dei Gonfaloni.

High altar, slabs of *Serravezza* framed in *Al. ametistino;* gradino of *Br. dor.;* four large borders beside doorway, *Rosso di Levanto*.

S. Lucia in Selci.—Rich tabernacle on the l. has fillet of *Cip. mand. rosso.*

S. Luigi.
On facciata, two salamanders, *Travertino* C.
Beside door at entrance, blotches of *Pav. cenerognolo* B.
Tomb to rt. of door, two cols *Rosso br.* B ; upper fillet, *Br. dor. oleosa* B.
5th left, two cols *Verde antico* C.
Lower plinth of opposite tomb, *Cor. policroma.*
3rd rt., snake below tomb on left wall, *Verde ran. fibroso* B.
4th rt., at modern tomb, *Br. di S. Ipolito grande.*
5th left, two large elliptical slabs on pavement, *P. santa reticolata* B (*rossa br.* R).
4th left, specchio of pilaster on rt., *Br. rossa lum.* B ; two cols *Giallo antico* C.
2nd left, two cols *Settebasi persichina* B ; 3rd and 4th balustri to left, *P. santa tigrata* S ; large slabs on pilasters, *Affr. verde rossastro.*
1st left, two cols *Cip. verde* C.

S. Marcello.
2nd rt., under altar, urn of *Porf. rosso* C.
4th rt., two cols *P. santa.*
High altar, urn of *Nero antico* C. Slab on pavement to rt. (Pietro Gilles), *Pario giallognolo* B.
4th left, two cols *Verde antico.*
3rd left, large slab on pavement, *Br. dor.* B.

S. Marco.
1st rt., gradino of *Pav. rossastro.* 1st Tomb has four pretty colonnettes of *P. santa*, varieties of *Giallo antico*, and central niche of *Cip. rosso.*
End of rt. aisle, tomb on steps, *Calcarea bigia;* in Chapel, two cols *Taormina br.;* on gradino, *P. santa br. min.* S; paliotto of *Al. orientale a nuvole* B (*cenerino fort.* R) bordered with *Tartaruga fior.;* specchi of *Al. tartaruga rosso.*
In chancel, four cols and urn, *Porf. rosso.;* pavement behind high altar, *Diaspro infimo.* Candlebearer, *Cor. policroma* B.

In Baptistery to left of door, urn of *Bigio br. ; pilasters of Pav. br. argentino.

S. M. degli Angeli.
1st Tomb on rt., large inscribed slab of Nero antico S.
2nd Tomb on left, two little squares below urn, Al. rossastro S.
2nd rt., two cols Br. pav. sfrangiata B.
4th rt., two cols Br. trac. C ; Br. polieroma B (Trac. gialla).
Specchi in choir, Cor. violetta (giallastra).
Two large slabs beside high altar, Cotognino a nuvole ; fillet of gradino, Settebasi pav. confusa.
Four large slabs outside chapel in left transept, Settebasi mand. B (pav. S). Opposite, in rt. transept, four of Serravezza mand.
1st left, two cols Giallo br. pall. ; balustri of Pav. tigrato S.

S. M. dell' Anima.
2nd rt., paliotto of *Semesanto giallo S ; enclosing bits of Verde ran. orbicolare. 4th rt., two cols Rosso di Francia.

S. M. in Aquiro.
3rd rt., four small bits under picture at entrance, Lum. di Egitto bigia B (gialla e bigia R).
2nd rt., two cols Br. rossa scura.

S. M. in Ara Coeli.
Tiny lozenge on pavement close to principal door, Gr. bigio min. confuso B.
Below Tomb on rt., small octagon of Br. di Simone S.
In nave, two fluted cols Tasio C.
Tiny square at foot of tomb, beyond the middle of nave, Cip. mand. verde min. S.
3rd rt., tomb on pavement, Lum. bigia S.
7th rt., *two cols Porf. verde R.
Tombs inside S. door, four small slabs, F. di Persico rossigno.
8th rt., on cancello, Br. Gregoriana S.
9th rt., four cols Pav. at tombs.
Tomb in l. corner of rt. trans., two oblongs of Br. trac. min. S ; eight specchi of Al. a rosa nuv. dor.
Rt. ambo, oblong slab on parapet to rt., Gr. verde confuso B.
10th rt., on cancello, Br. di Aleppo rossa ; gradino of Br. pav. S.

11th rt., two cols *Verde antico*.
Two large circular slabs at foot of chancel arch, *Porf. verde* B.
Tomb near high altar, two cols *P. santa*. Left col blotched with black.
11th left, two cols *Verde cupo*.
TEMPIETTO.—Eight cols *Broccatellone dor. (rosso e giallo)*.
10th left, two cols *Bianco e Nero (di Porto Ferrajo)*.
9th left, two cols **Br. trac. rossastra*.
8th left, two fluted cols *Giallo antico*.
7th left, two cols *Cor. rosea*; fillet and gradino, *Settebasi dor*. S.
6th left, two rounds on cancello, *Cip. rosso* (partly *pav. scuro* R).
5th left, paliotto of *Cor. rossa* S.
3rd left, balustri of *Al. rosso e giallo* S; *two cols *Br. dor.* C; fillet of *Br. pav. min.* S; pilasters of tabernacle, *Al. rossiccio* S.

S. M. in Campitelli.
Last left, fascia on paliotto *F. di Persico macchiato* S.

S. M. in Cappella.—Cols of *Cip.*, *Bigio br.*, and *Imezio*.

S. M. dei Cappuccini.
Small H. W. on each side, *Br. gialla e nera*.
High altar, two inter. cols *Tasio* C.

S. M. della Consolazione.
3rd rt., two cols *Nero strisciato (Bianco e nero di Porto Ferrajo)*.
End of rt. aisle, two small cols *Affr. pav.*; balustri, *Pav. bigio br.*
High altar, two cols *P. santa*.
4th left, on paliotto, *fillet of *Verde pall. br.*
2nd left, two cols *Bigio antico (scuro)*.
HOSPITAL.—Gradino of altar at end of main alley, *Cip. pav.*
Two pilasters at cancello, *Cip. mand. lionato chiaro* B; two (round the corner) *Lum. pav. disfatta* B.

S. M. in Cosmedin.
In portico, two fluted cols *Lesbio* C.
Rt. and left of door, spheres of *Nefritica bronzina*.
Cols in nave: one *Affr.*; one *Imezio*; one *Gr. rosso*; two *Tirio* C; two fluted *Pav.*; four *Bigio lum.*
Slab on rt. ambo, *Gr. della Sedia* S; square of *Cip. mand. verde giallastro* R (*min.* S).

Baldacchino, cols *Gr. rosso violaceo.*
CRYPT: two cols *Porino;* four *Gr. del Foro* C; slabs on pavement to left, *Greco ven.* S.
SACRISTY.—Two small tapering cols at tomb, *Giallo antico.*
S. M. in Domnica.
In front, ship of *Pentelico* C.
Paliotto rt., *Br. rossa.*
High altar, two cols *Porf. rosso;* frame of altar *Greco dislocato.*
Paliotto left, *Settebasi pav.*
S. M. Egiziaca.
Walls and several pillars, *Tufo rosso* B.
S. M. delle Grazie.
End of rt. aisle, two cols **Bigio br. scritto (chiaro);* on cancello **Pav. bigiastro reticolato.*
End of left aisle, two cols *Bigio mor.*
Cancello on left, four oblongs, *Br. di Aleppo.*
S. M. dell' Itria.
High altar, paliotto bordered with *F. di Persico* and *Diaspro rosso e giallo;* lower gradino, *Cor. pall. min.* Two small H. W., *P. santa cerulea.*
S. M. Liberatrice.
3rd rt., two cols *Cor. pall. (rossa e gialla* B).
High altar, two cols *Br. pav. bigiastra* B (*Serravezza antica*).
3rd left, two cols **Br. trac.;* on gradino, scraps of *Al. tartaruga.*
S. M. di Loreto.
High altar, two cols *Giallo picchiettato* B.
In Sacristy, two cols *Pav.,* two *Imezio.*
S. M. Maddalena.
Cancello 3rd rt., **Settebasi ven.* S.
S. M. Maggiore.
In portico, two cols **Gr. rosso verdastro;* one *Gr. del Foro;* one **Gr. bruno min.;* one **Gr. del Giglio macchiato;* forty-two cols in nave, *Imezio* B; altars and pilasters, *Imezio fasciato schietto.*
1st tomb rt., two cols **P. santa fasciata;* plinth of **Settebasi policroma.*

1st rt., two cols *Lum. degli Abruzzi* S.
BAPTISTERY.—Large tazza, *Porf. rosso*; two colonnettes, *Nero antico*; two cols *Verde antico*.
4th rt. (Crucifix), two slabs beside altar, *Sard. a rosa nuv.*
CAPP. SISTINA.—Eight cols *Verde pall.* On altar, large circle of *Gr. della Sedia*; below angels, **Al. ametista dend.*; **Porf. serp. verde*, **Semesanto min.*, agates and jaspers; below reliefs of tomb on rt., plinth of *Affr. sanguigno.*
Arch of papal throne, two slabs above and two crosses below, *Spato fluore* S.
CHOIR.—Baldacchino, cols and urn, *Porf. rosso*; **candlebearer, Bianco e nero antico* S.
[CAPP. BORGHESE.—Ten large pilasters *Broccatello principe* S.; at entrance to side chapels, *Broccatello pav. cupo* B.
Plinth of both tombs at base of eight cols (verde) *Rosso br. min.* S; specchi of *Al. fort.*; four large oblongs of *Al. melleo nuv.* B.
Four long slips under lower reliefs of tombs, *Settebasi policroma* S.
Frame of six black inscription slabs, *Al. a rosa fior.*
Fillet at base of altar, *Br. bianca e nera* B; broad fascia below cols, *Legno pietrificato.*
Plinth above floor all round the chapel, *Bardiglio fiorito list.*
In Sacristy, *two colonnettes, *Cotognino orientale* (broken); sfondi, *Br. Quintilina biancastra.*]
LEFT AISLE.—1st chapel, two cols *Verde pall.*; two *Affr.*, two **Bianco e nero dor.* (broken).
Two colonnettes at tomb, *Cor. giallastra* B (*violetta*).
Tomb of Card. Toledo, *two small oblongs, *Giallo tigrato* C; above inscription, fascia of *Br. rossa e gialla*; below, *Lum. degli Abruzzi* S.
1st tomb left, two cols *P. santa arlecchina*; plinth, *Rosso striato.*

S. M. sopra Minerva.

1st rt., two cols *Giallo br. bruno.*
2nd rt, on gradino, *Cip. marino* B (*nuv.* R); four circles of *Lum. gialla e pav.*, with ovals of **Diaspro rosso br.* and *Diaspro pav.*: below circles, oblongs of *Astracane giallo*; small triangles

Semesanto giallo S; on walls, *Lum. bigia* S; sfondi of *Lum. bigia di Egitto* S.

4th rt., fillets on tomb of Urban VII., *Rosso br. min.* S; paliotto, *Al. ad onice* S; two cols *Broccatellone;* balustri on left, *Pav. azzurrigno* B (*verdognolo*); on tomb to rt., *Semesanto pav.* S.

5th rt., four specchi at tomb, *Settebasi dor.*; two middle cols *Al. fior. list.* B; below cols, specchi of *Al. a pecorella* B; two cols *Occhio di Pav. pav.* B; four at tombs, *Verde cupo*: opposite, on 5th pilaster rt., two long corner strips at tomb, *P. santa fior.* S.

7th rt., four cols *Verde antico;* inner one on l., *Verde min.* B.

8th rt., two cols *Verde smeraldo* R.

9th rt., rt. col **Br. rossa e gialla*, l. col **Br. dor.*

Chapel to rt. of high altar, hexagons on pavement, *Palombino eburneo* B.

Left trans., border on pavement of large chapel, *Serp. violacea* B; two cols *Giallo br.*

Four cols *Verde antico.*

4th left, below cols, *F. di Persico bruniccio;* plinth of tomb, on the rt., *P. santa carnina* S.

3rd left, col on rt. *Cor. pav.*, left *P. santa.*

2nd left, two cols *P. santa bruna giallastra.*

Urn on left of main door (G. B. Galletto) *Cip. verde giallastro* B.

1st pilaster left, large fillets at tomb, *Br. pav.* S; plinth, *Pav. sanguigno* B.

Tomb at 1st pilaster left, four long narrow strips, *P. santa rossastra.*

In convent, frame of inscription at the top of library stairs, *Br. gialla.*

S. M. di Monserrato.

1st rt., two cols *Cor.*

2nd rt., two cols *Br. rossa.*

3rd rt., two cols *Giallo antico.*

1st left, band on paliotto, *P. santa giallastra br.* B; two cols *Verde di Ponsevera* (*Serp. cerulea* B).

S. M. in Monterone.

High altar, *two cols *Br. pav.*

3rd col rt., *Bigio br.*

S. M. di Monte Santo.
2nd l., gradino of *Settebasi pav.* and *Trac. violetta min.*
3rd l., below cols, *specchi of *Al. cip.*; on the rt., door of *Sard. nuv.* framed in *Al. ametista dend.*

S. M. ai Monti.
H. W., *Rosso br. min.*
1st rt., two cols *P. santa.*
2nd rt. and left, two large octagons on pavement in front, *Br. rossa e gialla frantumata* B.
2nd rt., two cols *Giallo dor.*
High altar, two cols *P. santa*; col on rt. has a handsome patch of Breccia in the middle.
2nd left, two cols *Verde antico*: cancello, *P. santa bigia* B (*fior.*).
1st left, two cols *Affr.*

S. M. in Monticelli.
High altar, two large cols *Verde chiaro.*

S. M. dell' Orazione.
2nd left, gradino of *Br. trac.*; the finest in Rome for brilliancy, minuteness, and variety.

S. M. dell' Orto.
3rd rt., two cols *Bigio lum.*
High altar, two cols *Affr. fior.*
4th left, col on l., *Giallo bigiastro*; on rt., *Giallo br.*: four oblongs on cancello, *Cor. rossastra dor.*
2nd left, on cancello, *Cor. schietta.*

S. M. della Pace.
3rd rt., slab on pavement, *Settebasi dor.* S.; on cancello, four oblongs of *Br. min. angolosa.*
Pilasters outside 4th rt., *Broccatello rosso*: outside chancel, *Broccatello giallo* S.
High altar, four cols *Verde antico*; lowest plinth of *Lum. nera di Etiopia* S; four slabs on walls, *P. santa gialla cerulea* S; 2nd left, slabs of *Affr. rossastro* on arch and outer walls.

S. M. del Popolo.
Tomb at H. W. on rt., fillet under moulding, and two strips below, *Cip. rosso.*

High altar, four inter. cols *Porto Venere*; below cols, ovals of *Sard. a rosa* on *Al. marino dor.*

Narrow fillet four feet from the ground, *Br. policroma* R (*sanguigna*); two pilastrini of cancello, *Lum. bigia rossastra.*

Tomb between 3rd and 4th left, two long vertical strips of *Cip. mand. rosso.*

2nd left, on cancello, *Giallo br.*; middle slab of entrance piers, **Br. dor.*

S. M. della Scala.

2nd rt., paliotto of *Pav. br. dor.* S, framed in **Bigio mor. ad Occhi.*

4th rt., on gradino, *Diaspro giallo.*

High altar, fillets of *Settebasi dor.*; many lastre of *Al. a tartaruga* S.

4th left, two cols *Br. di Simone*; on specchi, two ovals of *Al. onichino* S; on gradino, *Lum. gialla e pav.*, **Settebasi pav.*, and **Astracane giallo.*

1st left, on cancello, *P. santa br.* S; two figures on gradino, *Br. trac.* S.

S. M. del Sole.

Seventeen fluted cols *Pario* C. Basement and steps, *Tufo rosso* B.

S. M. in Traspontina.

1st rt., two strips beside cols, *Palombara fasciato*; cornice of gradino, *Settebasi pav. angolosa* B.

2nd rt., on side walls, border of *Rosso br. min.*

3rd rt., two cols *Bigio mor. ondulato* R; four specchi below cols *F. di Persico rosso*; fillet on gradino, *Br. pav. verdiccia* B.

5th l., on cancello, **Giallo br. principe.*

Rt. trans., below cols, two slabs of *Al. a pecorella pall.*

High altar, border of arms in front on pavement, *Lum. gialla di Egitto* B; 3rd left, two cols *P. santa*; 2nd left, on gradino, **Al. melleo rossiccio* B.

S. M. in Trastevere.

Several cols in nave, *Gr. del Foro bicolore* S; 8th col rt., *Gr. rosso fasciato* R.

Cornice of tomb to rt. of door, *Cor. pall.* S (*rosea*).

End of rt. aisle in a niche, three spheres of *Nefritica*; one of *Occhio di Pav. rosso* B.
Urn below altar of closed chapel, *Bianco e Nero tigrato*.
Baldacchino cols *Porf. rosso*.
6th left, two cols *Broccatellone* (*pav*.) B; below, *Br. gialla*; on cancello, *Br. gialla rossastra* S.
5th left, two cols *Affr. bigio*.
3rd and 2nd left, two cols *Al. bruno*.
2nd left, gradino of *Br. gialla* S.
1st left, two cols *Affr. nero*.

S. M. in Trevi.
2nd left, two small cols *Verde antico*.

S. M. dell' Umiltà.
1st rt., on side walls, strips of *Br. marrone* S.
2nd rt., on gradino, *Sard. a rosa nuv.
High altar, two cols *Giallo br.*

S. M. delle Vergini.
1st left, on upper gradino, *Settebasi dor.* S; two cols *Bianco e nero di Francia*.

S. M. in Via.
1st rt., two cols *Pav. br.*
2nd rt., two cols *Broccatellone*; sfondi of *Settebasi dor.*
4th rt., on paliotto, *Cor. brunastra*.
4th left, two cols *P. santa ven.*
3rd left, *two cols *Br. trac.*; picture framed in *Astracane giallo*.
2nd left, two cols *P. santa reticolata*; paliotto of *Br. verde*.
1st left, two cols *Giallo br.*; on cancello, inner oblongs *Bianco e nero antico*; outer, *Bianco e nero di Francia*.

S. M. in Via Lata.
End chapels, rt. and left, moulded frames of *Occhio di Pav. rosso*; plinths of *Pav. br. argentino*.
Pavement in choir, four octagonal slabs of *Lum. bigia orientale* R.
Tomb to left of door, *Cip. verd. chiaro* spoilt by splaying; arched border, *Verde di Ponsevere chiaro* S.

S. M. della Vittoria.

1st rt. on cancello, outer pilaster, *Br. rossa poligonia* R; inner, *Cor. min.* (*pall.*) B; three other slabs, *Cor. rossa* ; two cols *Taormina* on plinth of *Br. rossa* ; border of two ovals on gradino, *Lum. bigia di Egitto* S; centre of specchi below cols, *Al. tartaruga giallastro* S; on pilasters of arch, four slabs of *Br. Quintilina biancastra* ; rounds and ovals of *Agata rossa* ; two long vertical slips of *Settebasi giallastra* on corner pilasters beside cols.

2nd rt., two cols *Giallo ven.;* on pavement, close to the altar, *Affr. rosso conchigliare* S; on gradino, two oblongs of *Al. tartaruga pall.* : high up inside pilasters of arch, two borders of **Affr. rosso.*

3rd rt., cancello and gradino, *Al. a rosa list.* S; lowest slab of entrance pilasters, *P. santa arlecchina;* outside cancello, two long vertical strips of *Giallo di Siena ven.* (flushed).

High altar, cancello, *Pav. br.*; five slabs on pavement, *P. santa a Stuoia;* door-jambs, *Br. di Aleppo;* moulding on the rt., *Trac. min.*

4th left, 1st col left, *Affr. pav.* B; 2nd left, *Affr. verde* B; 2nd rt., *Affr. verde bigiastro* R; on cancello, *Giallo paglino* B; plinth, *Serravezza pav.*; gradino of *Br. policroma* ; fillet above altar, *Settebasi dor.*; two horizontal slabs by altar, *Al. fort. lum.* ; two vertical slabs, *Al. orientale a nuvole* B; sham doors, *Sard. orientale list.* S.

3rd left, on cancello, *Br. rossa min.*; two long vertical strips of *P. santa rossa br.* S; col on left, *Giallo carnagione;* on rt., *Giallo dor. piritifero* R, both fluted; picture framed in **Al. brunastro ond.;* inside pilasters of arch, *Br. trac. chiara*, enclosing lozenges of *Al. dor.*; centre of gradino, *Legno pietrificato verde*, between bits of *Diaspro rosso dend.*; rounds and ovals of *Agata rossa*.

2nd left, fillet above gradino, *Al. fort.*; plinth under cols, *Palombara violetto.*

1st left, centre of gradino and ovals on specchi, *Al. onichino* S; gradino, *Semesanto giallo* S; at each end of gradino, *Al. a rosa;* on cancello, four oblongs of *Verde picchiettato;* high up on pilasters of arch, *Settebasi gialla*, mixed with *F. di Persico*; lowest border of pilasters, *P. santa rossa reticolata* S; on paliotto, *Semesanto pav.*

S. Martina.—High altar, four cols *Al. bruno pall. ond* (see *S. Luca*).

S. Martino.

Two cols *Cip.*; six *Pav.*; ten *Imezio*; six *Bigio antico*; 4th and 5th left, *B. azzurrognolo* B.

End of left aisle, gradino of *Al. fort. occhiuto* S, bordered with *F. di Persico*; mouldings round the altar, *Diaspro rosso*.

High altar, four slabs *Gr. della Sedia*: in crypt, sphere of *Nefritica bronzina*.

Sacristy, col of *Gr. persichino*.

S. Michele in Borgo.—Tomb on left, plinth of *Rosso br. min.* S; four lastrine of *Al. rosso e giallo list.*

S. Michele a Ripa.

Candlebearer, *P. santa br.*

SS. Nereo ed Achilleo.

Altar rt. and l., two spiral cols *Pav. bianco*: *specchi of *Giallo br. dor.*; two candlebearers, *Pav. ven.*

Cols of Baldacchino: three *Affr. verde*, one *Affr. nero*; on screen, twenty-four panels, *Porf. rosso*; beside chair, two spiral cols *Porino*.

Stem of pulpit, *Affr. bronzato*; six ovals, *Al. mellco fior.*

S. Niccolò degli Arcioni.

Cancello of high altar, four narrow slabs, *Br. Gregoriana* S; two wide, *Settebasi pav. fior.* S.

S. Niccolò in Carcere.

3rd col rt., *Cip. verde increspato* B.

Baldacchino cols, *Cotognino orientale ven.*; urn of *Porf. verde* B.

In confession, two cols *P. santa bigia*; two, *P santa rossa br.* B.

3rd col left, *Cip. verde zonale* united with *Cip. prasio* B.

1st col left, *Greco scritto* B (*tratteggiato* R).

S. Niccolò dei Prefetti.

2nd rt., *two cols *Pav. bruno* B (*scuro angoloso*).

S. Niccolò ai Cesarini.

Pillars of *Tufo rosso* C.

S. Niccolò da Tolentino.
Frame of tomb on pavement by the entrance, *Bigio mor. orbicolare* B.
Under organ, four cols *Serravezza persichina.*
1st rt., oblong slab on pavement, *Gr. della Colonna* S; paliotto, *Al. bianco a nuvole* S; on cancello, *Diaspro verde.*
3rd rt., two squares beside cols, *Settebasi dor.* S; two small borders on gradino, *Semesanto giallo* S; four narrow strips in sfondi, *Palombara rosso list.* S.
4th rt. and left, and at high altar, *eight fluted cols *Bardiglio.*
Border on side walls of choir, *Occhio di Pav. pav.* S.
2nd left, six cols *Verde antico* C; specchi below cols. *Bianco e nero min.* S; feet of urns, *Verde ran. scuro* S.

S. Onofrio.
H. W., stem and foot, chased *Pentelico.*
Cancello on rt., *Pav. bianco ven.* S.
2nd rt., two cols *Broccatellone*; beside tombs, four specchi of *Al. a rosa confuso;* outside the chapel, four narrow strips of *Settebasi dor.;* four bits on inner pilasters, *Lum. bigia di Egitto;* four on outer, *Lum. gialla di Egitto.*
High altar, on cancello, two lastre of *Al. a rosa ven.*; scraps on altar, *Semesantone rosso, Br. di Aleppo,* and many good alabasters; on tabernacle, six tiny oblongs of *Br. di S. Ipolito.*
Balustrini of cancello at sides, *P. santa pav. intrecciata.*
4th left, gradino of *Lum. rossa.*
1st left, six splayed slabs of *Spato fluore list.;* eight oblongs of *Semesantone pav.* Urn of *Sardonico chiaro* framed in *Verde di Ponsevere chiaro;* gradino of *Al. di Civitavecchia.*
Tomb on l. of door, narrow strip above, *Lum. nera di Etiopia* R.
In cloister, cols of *Lesbio* C.

S. Pancrazio.
On the left, large fluted and thrice moulded col of *Pav.* with capital.
Baldacchino cols *Porf. rosso.* Beside the high altar, four cols *Gr. bigio;* good scraps of *Cip.* and *Pav.;* two specchi of *Lumachellone bigio.*
Two spiral jewelled candlebearers with balls of *P. santa;* plinth of porphyry urn, *Bigio intrecciato* B.

S. Pantaleo.

Tomb in middle of pavement, four thistle leaves of *Serp. tigrata* S.
Pilasters of choir, *P. santa rossastra conchigliare* S ; urn of *Porf. rosso.*
Lower gradino and tabernacle, *Al. ametista S (*dend.*) ; cancello of *Affr. sanguigno.*

S. Paolo fuori le Mura.

Four cols at W. entrance, *Cip. verde.*
Floor of nave, *Bardiglio list. (scuro R).*
Forty large and forty smaller cols, *Gr. del Sempione* C.
Four cols at baldacchino and two at W. door, *Cotognino orientale* B; plinth of *Br. verde di Egitto.*
Inner baldacchino, four cols *Porf. rosso;* specchi of *Lapis lazzuli scuro* and *Malachite.*
Two slabs in front of high altar, *Porf. serp. verde cupo.*
Confession, above the altar, *Settebasi pav.* S; pilasters of apse and transept, *Pav. policromo* R; four fluted cols **Pav. tigrato*, saved from the fire.
On floor of apse, *two large circles of *Lumachellone antico* B; two of the smallest, *Br. pav. livida* B; on walls, *Cip. zonale.*
In transepts, eight slabs of *Rosso antico* framed in *Verde di Grecia.*
TRANSEPT CHAPELS, beginning on the left:—
I. Two cols *Porf. rosso;* on walls, *Settebasi pav. fior.*
II. On cancello, *Br. dor.;* beside urn, specchi of **Settebasi cupo:* Rich altar has colonnettes of *Broccatello* and *Cip. rosso.*
III. Two cols *Porf. rosso;* narrow sfondo on rt., *Diaspro rosso br.;* gradino and plinth of cols, *Trac. angolosa* B.
IV. Twelve fluted Doric cols **Bigio chiaro;* paliotto and sides of altar, *Palombara (*dend.*) *erbor.* B.
Portico of N. transept, twelve cols *Imezio.*

S. Paolo alla Regola.

Fillet on rt., **Affr. violetto;* pedestal on left, **Bianco e nero di Egitto.*

S. Paolo alle Tre Fontane.

At altar, rt. and left, two cols *Broccatellone* C.

Below cols on left, *Al. a pecorella* : at fountain niches, six cols *Affr.* C: central head, *Giallo solforato*; plinth of *Cip. verde rigato* (see S. Vincenzo and Scala Coeli).

S. PIETRO IN VATICANO.

Front of *Travertino di Tivoli* B.

PORTICO, two cols *Pav. br.*; two *Affr. bigio* [foot of col on rt., *Affr. nero ondato* B; left, *Affr. nero quarzifero* B].

Two cols *Gr. dendritico*: two *Gr. bigio*; two *Gr. rosso*: two *Gr. del Foro*; eight *Cip. verde ondato* R; at main doorways, six inter. cols *Pav.* Jambs of Porta santa, *P. S. bigia* B.

Borders of slabs on pavement near entrance, *Br. rossa e gialla.*

Forty-four cols *Cottanello giallo* B; on piers, *Rosso di Fr.*

Chapels.—PIETÀ, on rt., spiral col *Tirio.*

S. SEBASTIANO.—Two large three-quarter cols *P. san'a fior.*; on cancello, *Al. rosso e giallo, Bianco e nero antico*, and *Diaspro verdastro rigato.*

Tomb of Inn. XII., door-jambs and cornice, *Giallo br. dor.* B.

SAGRAMENTO.—Two spiral cols, *Tirio* C; doves on four piers in front of chapel, framed in *Bigio macchiato scuro*.

MADONNA.—Cols of *Bigio br.*, enclosing two of *Verde antico*: slabs on pilasters of arch *Al. a rosa ranciato* B: picture frame and middle of arch, *Spato fluore* S.

S. GIROLAMO (opposite the altar).—Two three-quarter cols *Cip.*: on cancello, *Al. melleo rossiccio.*

ST. BASIL, and at adjacent tombs of Gregory XVI. and Benedict XIV., six cols *Bigio antico* (three patched with *Affr.*).

ST. WENCESLAUS.—Two cols of *Gr. rosso*, enclosing two of *Giallo br. pall. rossastro*; on walls, ovals of *Settebasi bigia.*

SS. PROCESSO E MARTINIANO.—*Two inter. cols of *Giallo antico*, enclosing two of *Porf. rosso scuro*; specchi of *F. di Persico min.*, and oblongs of *Affr. schiacciato.*

ERASMUS.—Two cols of *Gr. rosso*, enclosing two of *Giallo br. pall. rossastro*; four small ovals on arch, *Br. pav. sfrangiata* B; on cancello, *P. santa fiorita.*

Tomb of Clement XIII., plinth of *Calcarea bigia*.

S. MICHELE.—Two cols of *Gr. del Foro*, enclosing *two of *P. santa bicolore* (*ven.*); eight lunettes on arch, divided by crosses, *Br. pav. min.* B; specchi of *Pal. list.*; corner pilasters at side of cancello, *Br. rossa*.

S. PETRONILLA.—Col on rt., *Gr. del Foro*; left, *Gr. rossastro*; eight slabs at foot of arch, *Al. a pecorella min.* B (*dor.* R).

TABITHA.—Two cols *Gr. persichino*.

Slab on each side of bronze sitting statue, *Gr. della Sedia* B.

Below cupola, eight spiral cols *Tirio* C. On walls, pilasters of *Diaspro tenero*; pavement, *Diaspro infimo*.

Confession.—Four cols, *Al. a nuvole* C; inside cancello, eight lastre of *Semesanto giallo*; on stairs, eight *Rosso br.*; on walls, eight *Al. onichino*.

Colonnettes sustaining small statues of SS. Peter and Paul, **Al. di Orte*.

Crypt.—Sixteen cols *Br. pav. ven.* C.

End of **tribune**, four cols *I mezio zonale*; plinth of *Br. pav. grande*. Tomb of Paolo III., mask of *Giallo e nero antico* C.

M. DELLA COLONNA.—Two cols *Gr. del Foro arrugginito*; two *Giallo solforato*; plinth of cols *Pav. turc.* B; above altar, *Al. rosso e giallo* S.

SAPPHIRA.—Two cols *Gr. persichino*; near middle of pier on rt., **Occhio di Pav. rosso*.

S. TOMMASO.—Two cols *Cip. verde*; two *Bigio mor. dor.*

S. PIETRO.—Rt. col *Giallo antico*; left **Giallo dor.* B; two cols *Porf. rosso*.

S. FRANCESCO.—Two cols *Gr. del Foro*; two *Bigio mor.*

SS. SIMON AND JUDE: on the rt., two long narrow strips, *Br. pav. trac. min.* B; upper gradino, *Settebasi rossa* R.

Sacristy.—At doorway, two cols *Gr. del Foro*; on projecting pier to left, 3rd slab from the bottom, **Giallo sfrangiato*; pier to rt. of it framed in *P. santa bigia dor.*

In passage, splayed pilasters of *Pav. br. dor.* S.

Four cols *Gr. rosso*; two *Gr. del Foro*; sixteen *Bigio antico*; twelve fluted *Bigio lum.*

Pilasters on walls, *Giallo di Siena;* slabs below pilasters, *Cip. verde chiaro* and *C. bigio;* beyond glass door, *two cols *Bigio mor.;* in passage, pilasters of *Affr. bigio* and *A. verde.*
In chapel, mass of *Cristallo iridato.* Two inter. cols, *Al. bianco.*
On left of entrance, fluted col of *Bigio br. macchiato.*
Tomb of *Cip. nero.*
GREGORIANA.—*Two cols *Porf. bigio;* two, *Verde antico.*
On cancello, five lastre of *Br. di Simone;* upper gradino, *Settebasi policroma* B.
Tomb of Pius VII.—Two cols *Gr. persichino;* on piers at side, four circles of *Verde pall. min.*
TRANSFIGURATION opposite, two cols *Cip.*
Tomb of Inn. XI., *Cip. nero* S.
  Choir.—*Candlebearer of *Bianco e nero antico;* bands on arch outside Choir, *P. santa madreporitica* B.
PRESENTATION.—Col on rt., *P. santa bigia* B ; left, *P. santa rossa* B.
  Baptistery.—Large font of *Porf. rosso.*

SS. Pietro e Marcellino.

Two inter. cols *Cottanello* at each side altar, and urns of *Verde antico.*
S. Pietro in Montorio.
4th rt., alternate balustri of *Giallo antico* and *Pav.*
3rd left, balustri of *Pav. br.* and two oblongs of *Giallo br.;* two small cols *Porto Venere ven.*
S. Pietro in Vincoli.—Twenty fluted cols *Imezio.*
Cancello, end of rt. aisle, *Br. di Simone;* long strip below tomb beyond 1st rt., *Cor. violetta giallastra* S.
In sacristy, *slabs of *Porf. serp. verde,* and *Porf. rosso.*
On high altar, paliotto of *Al. onichino* bound with *Semesanto,* and flanked with *Br. verde di Egitto min.;* borders of *Giallo carnagione tigrato.*
On walls of confession, *Br. di Aleppo, Rosso antico, Al. a pecorella;* on each side of steps, sloping fillet of *Rosso br.;* below, two small triangles, *Br. dor.;* on pavement, *Cip. mand.;* below statues, two small bits of *Cip. rosso.*

End of left aisle, two cols *Bigio ven.* C ; on walls, *Pav. br. dor.* S ; on cancello, *F. di Persico macchiato* S.

2nd tomb left, *two slabs *Al. a rosa* ; fillet below inscription, *Br. pav.* S.

1st tomb left, urn of *Sard. scuro.*

S. Prassede.

1st tomb on rt., two cols *Broccatelloue giallo.*

2nd rt., on pilasters of arch, *Palombara fasciato* B.

3rd rt., col on rt., outside, **Porf. serp. nero* B ; col on left, outside, and large col on rt., within, **Gr. bianco e nero* B.

Col on left, within, *Gr. nero tigrato* C. Two cols *Gr. bigio;* two small spirally fluted cols, *Al. bruno rossastro.*

High altar, four cols *Porf. rosso :* *candlebearer of *Serravezza ;* six chased cols *Pentelico* C.

Fourteen steps, *Russo antico* ; cancello, *Cor. violacea dor.* R.

Below choir, col of *Gr. della colonna* B.

Sacristy: oval on paliotto, *Porf. rosso pomato* S.

4th left, two cols *Porf. rosso.*

3rd left, two cols *Al. orientale onichino* B.

1st left, paliotto of *F. di Persico pav.* S.

1st and 5th col, left, *Gr. violetto* R.

Slab on wall to left of main door, *Bianco e nero tigrato.*

S. Prisca.

At door, left col of *Gr. persichino.*

High altar, col on left, *Br. rossa* ; rt., **Cor. grande.*

S. Pudenziana.

Stem of H. W. on rt., *Affr. nero.*

2nd rt., balustri of cancello, *Pav. sanguigno confuso.*

Pavement at end of each aisle, small squares of *Palombino bianco.*

2nd left, two cols *Bigio ven.*

1st left, four cols *Giallo antico* ; four *Verde antico ;* two urns. **Giallo e nero antico ;* oblongs above statues of Virtues. *Br. policroma* B ; on wall, narrow strips, *Br. Quintilina.*

Two large cols *Lum. degli Abruzzi :* plinth and upper gradino. *Br. di Aleppo ;* lower gradino, *Serravezza :* on altar, four *slabs, *Al. a rosa.*

Ovals beside tomb, *Sard. giallo e rosso ; urn of Br. gialla e nera ; under crosses on three hillocks of Verde di Firenze, oblong slabs of Br. pav. min.

Pilasters at entrance arch, framed in F. di Persico reticolato.

SS. Quattro Coronati.
2nd left, two cols P. santa.

High altar, on cancello, *Al. melleo nuv. ; on pavement, Occhio di Pav. pav.

S. Rocco.
5th rt., two inter. cols Taormina ; below them, *Al. a tartaruga.

Two urns, Bianco e nero tigrato ; *plinth below them, Giallo nuv.

On the walls, Al. occhiuto and Al. fort.

3rd rt., two cols Rosso di Levanto, on *plinth of Cip. verde chiaro.

Crucifix framed in Verde di Grecia ; gradino, Lum. rossa ; below, two small oblongs of Rosso br.

S. Saba.
Base of 1st col, rt. and left, Porf. verde B.

High altar, *two outside cols Gr. bianco e nero ; *two inside, Bianco e nero di Egitto.

1st oblong slab in upper row to left, *Porf. nero grafico.

S. Sabina.
Twenty-four fluted cols Imezio ; sphere of Nefritica bruna B.

Tomb on rt., plinth of Bigio br. min.

2nd rt., two cols Al. melleo fior. ; two P. santa a Stuoia.

Chapel on left, pilasters beside picture, Verde picchiettato ; gradino of Br. trac. min. ; plinth under cols Affr. lum. ; tomb-slabs framed in Diaspro verde e giallo. Outside the chapel, two long vertical strips of Greco dislocato.

1st tomb left, two small cols Verde chiaro.

At main door, four spiral cols Pav.

S. Salvatore in Lauro.
Two large H. W. Serp. moschinata R (verde B) ; two large lozenges on pavement, Br. trac. violetta min. S.

2nd rt., on paliotto, Al. a pecorella list. ; on walls, Al. orientale oleoso B ; sfondi, Al. rosso e giallo S ; two pilasters of Br.

rossa ; opposite, two of *Br. rossa min.*; gradino, *Cip. rosso* ; eight strips of *Lum. bigia giallastra*.
Four H. W., *P. santa bigia nuv.* S.
High altar, balustri of *Pav. azzurrigno* B (*bruno* R). In both transepts, cols of **Cip. verde* ; specchi, *P. santa lum.*
In Cloister, twelve cols *Cip.*, six *Porino*, eight *Bigio antico*.
2nd left, on cancello, balustri of *Affr. bigio scuro*.
1st left on cancello, two pilastrini of *Al. rosso e giallo* S.

S. Salvatore.—Near high altar, col of *Bigio antico* C.

S. Salvatore in Onda.
**Baldacchino cols, *P. santa alabastrina* : cancello, *Verde di Grecia*.
Cancello on left, *Affr. disfatto*.

S. Sebastiano (fuori le Mura).
1st rt., two small cols *Affr. pezzato*. Relics framed in *Al. a rosa*.
1st tomb rt., plinth below urn, *Rosso br. lum*.
3rd rt., on walls, *Br. di Serravezza* (*Br. pav. bianca*) and *Giallo carnagione* B ; door frames, *Sard. orientale scuro* ; fillets and mouldings behind altar, *F. di Persico violetto* ; wreath at credence tables, *Verde di Susa*.
High altar, three cols *Verde antico* (extreme l., *V. pall.*); moulded frame of fresco, *Giallo br. pall.* On cancello, *Al. a rosa dend.*

S. Sebastiano in Pallara.
High altar, col on left, *Br. rossa*.

S. Silvestro in Capite.
High altar : at tabernacle, *four inter. colonnettes *Giallo antico*.

S. Silvestro al Quirinale.
Tomb at end wall of nave, two cols of *Serp. rosso* (*Rosso di Levanto*). Fillet below relief of Baptism, *Al. a rosa*, with scraps of *Br. Quintilina*.
1st rt., two cols *Affr. nero* C ; on entrance arch, four ovals of *Semesantone pav.*
Altar framed in **Pav. br.*; specchi below cols, *F. di Persico rosso* : *fillet of *Al. a rosa* ; small urn of *Serp. fior.*
Six large slabs, *Al. fior. list.* S ; eight small ovals, *Al. rosso*.
2nd rt., on entrance arch, fillet of *Affr. sanguigno* ; four oblongs, *Al. rosso e giallo list.* Two small cols *Al. di Montauto*.

2nd rt. and left, on paliotto, *P. santa rossa br.
2nd left, plinth and fillet, Settebasi dor. S ; gradino, Al. a rosa : two cols Taormina : behind cols, strips of Al. ametista dend.
1st left, entrance pilasters, Al. a rosa on Giallo focato ; paliotto of Cotognino a nuvole.

SS. Simone e Giuda.
Paliotto of altars, rt. and left, circles of Lum. di Calabria S, spoilt by red monogram.

S. Sisto.
Slab on left of door, framed in Cor. pall. ven.
In the oratory, two cols Gr. rosso ; two Gr. bigio.

S. Spirito (Via Giulia).
2nd left, two cols Broccatello pav. cupo.

S. Spirito in Sassia.
Cancello of nine side altars, *Br. trac. pav. rossastra S.
1st rt., specchi of Al. rosso nuv.
Col on rt., Affr. pav. B ; left, Affr. rosso. Four cols on rt., under organ, Gr. carnicino grigiastro B. (Gr. minuto carnicino chiaro R).
5th left, *two cols Bigio cupo macchiato.
1st left, two cols, mixed P. santa rossa and P. S. bigia orbicolare B ; below cols, broad fascia Br. rossa.
HOSPITAL : at altar, two cols Pav. br. C ; gradino of Palombara dend.
Pilasters and frieze of fountain in Court, Verde ran. ond. B.
Door-jambs of Spezieria, *Bigio br. B.

S. Stanislao.—*Fillet at all four altars, Br. trac. min.

S. Stefano del Cacco.
6th col rt., *Pav. br. ; 4th Cip. bigio ; 1st Cip. verde.
2nd left, on paliotto, scraps of Verde ran. macchiato, Cip. mand. verde, and Semesanto pav. S ; specchi of Broccatello giallo ; below, slabs of Astracane giallo.
1st left, fascia of Settebasi rossastra : two cols Diaspro verde.

S. Stefano dei Mori.
Behind the Church, two cols Cip.

S. Stefano Rotondo.
2nd left, tomb framed in *Affr. verde*; fascia above, *Settebasi bigia* S; slab in the middle, *Bigio scritto reticolato*.
2nd left, urn of *Giallo antico* C.
1st left, *Diaspro rosso list.* and *D. verde*: moulding of *Bigio list.*

S. Susanna.
Door-jambs at entrance, *Greco dislocato* B.
Two ovals on face of chancel arch, *Br. trac. rossa* B (*Br. policroma rossastra* S); two oblongs of *Cor. rossa* S.
Four slabs in corners of apse, facing the altar, *Br. pav. reticolata* S; plinth below chancel arch, and cancello, *Settebasi bruna giallastra*.
In semi-crypt, two cols *Tasio* C.
Chapel to left, large slabs on walls, *Br. dorata* S; Chigi arms, *Al. pomato* S; four square slabs, *Verde br.*: two oblongs, *F. di Persico chiaro*; two cols *Verde antico*.
At Convent door, two cols *Pentelico* C.

S. Teodoro.
On cancello, six bits of *Cip. verde ond.*

S. Tommaso ai Cenci.
Four disks on pavement, *Porf. rosso* and *Porf. serp. verde*.
In upper Oratory, gradino of *Br. rossa*.

S. Tommaso in Formis.
High altar, four *fluted cols *Pav. argentino reticolato*.
Picture framed in *Broccatellone*.

S. Urbano.
In front, four fluted cols *Bigio antico*.

S. Venanzio.
—Four lastre on cancello, *Affr. nero br.*: four *Cotognino a nuvole*.

SS. Vincenzo ed Anastasio (Trevi).
2nd left, fillet under cornice of altar, and sfondi, *Br. di S. Ipolito*.

S. Vincenzo ed Anastasio (Tre Fontane).
Four cols in portico, *Gr. bigio*.

S. Vitale.
1st rt., col on rt., *Bigio lum. chiaro*; l., *Cip. bigio*.
Gradino of four altars, *Cip. mand.*

High altar, two cols of *Porto Venere*: paliotto, *Al. nuv. bruno*; mouldings of *Pav. argentino*.

1st left, col on left, *Bigio ven.*; col on rt., *Cip. bigio*.

S. Vito.
Inscribed slab to rt. of altar on the rt., *Inezio*.

Scala Coeli.
Two cols *P. santa cerulea*: stem of H. W., *F. di Persico* (*ven.*).

In crypt, two cols *Lesbio*; on shelf in niche, *Nefritica bruna* (*nera*).

Stimmate.
Altar frames and mouldings, *Al. di Montauto nuvolato*.

Suffragio.
1st rt., plinth below specchi of cols, *Occhio di pernice S.

2nd rt., narrow fillet of *Settebasi dor. S.*

3rd rt., two cols *Serravezza pav.*

High altar, four slabs on gradino, *Pav. bigio br.*; plinth below cols *Settebasi pav.*; lower gradino, *Fiore di Persico br.*

1st left, *two cols *Affr. pav. giallastro*: fillet of *Br. pav. bruna* B.

Trinità dei Monti.
4th rt., two cols *P. santa*.

7th rt., two cols *Bigio ven.*

5th left, two cols *P. santa ven.*

3rd left, on paliotto, *Cotognino orientale*.

2nd left, on paliotto, *Affr. nero sanguigno*.

1st left, on paliotto, *Lum. degli Abruzzi*.

Trinità dei Pellegrini.
2nd rt., two cols *Cor. pall.*; *gradino, *Bigio lum*.

3rd rt., two cols *Verde di Pousevera*.

High altar, *four cols *Affr.*; *gradino of *Palombara rigato*.

4th left, two cols *Porto Venere*: *specchi of *Al. ouichino fior.*; at sides, *two slabs, *Lum. nera*.

3rd left, two cols *P. santa*; two slabs on pilasters, *Astracane bruno*; two oblongs, *A. giallo*.

2nd left, *two cols *Giallo nuv.*

HOSPICE: door-jambs of Refectory on ground floor, *Cip. mand. lionato* B.

Oratorio di S. Giovanni.
At high altar, *two cols *Giallo di Siena dor.*
Ospedale di S. Giovanni.
At altar, two cols *Cor. policroma* B (*rossa e gialla*).
Pantheon.
Seven cols in portico, *Gr. bigio del Foro* B (partly *rosco*).
Pilasters at doorway, *Tasio* C.
Door-jambs and capitals, *Lunense* B ; pavement at doorway, *Affr. rosso* B (*conchigliare*).
2nd rt., paliotto of *Palombara pav.*; at chapels, eight small fluted cols *Giallo br.*
Six cols *Pav. tigrato.*
5th altar, rt. and left, two cols *Porf. rosso cupo.*
Candlebearer, *Cip. bigio.*
Scala Santa.
Steps of *Tirio* C (*Greco turchiniccio* B); 5th step, typical.
SANCTA SANCTORUM, two cols *Porf. rosso* C.
CHAPEL on the rt., at the top of the stairs, on paliotto and in centre of gradino, *Cip. pav. scuro*, ruined by splaying.
Middle of paliotto, *Verde picchiettato ;* two oblongs of *Al. tartaruga brunastro ;* on cancello, two *slabs, *Affr. disfatto.*
Tor de' Specchi.
In Chapel, cancello of *Settebasi bigia.*
Cloaca Maxima.—Mouth of *Sperone* C.
Collegio Romano.
Large block of *Serp. granatite* C ; Cameo of Savonarola, *Niccolo* C ; buckles of *Agata zaffirina* C ; engravings of Polymnia, *Corniola* C ; triangular fragment of Clessida, with five hieroglyphics, *Gr. corallino minuto* B ; trunk of a small Egyptian idol, covered with hieroglyphics, *Gr. verde ucreggiante* B.
Colosseum: Large blocks of *Travertino di Tivoli* B.
Fontana dei Termini.—Rt. col, *Settebasi verde* B.
Forum of Nerva.—Three *fluted cols *Tasio* C.
Forum Romanum.
Fluted col of Phocas; *Lunense* C.
Temple of Concord: slab on pavement, *Affr. rosso br.* B.

Temple of Vespasian ; Temple of Castor and Pollux : three fluted cols *Lunense* C.

Forum of Trajan.—Many broken cols of *Gr. del Foro*.

Kircherian Museum (see *Collegio Romano*).

Lateran Museum.—Room II., flattened sphere of *Nefritica nera*. IV., large *Vase of *Bigio rossastro lum.* on stem of *Affr.* V., Stag in *Basalte macchiato;* Cow in *Lunense.* IX., two large sculptured cols, and a smaller one, of *Tasio* C. X., *two cols *Astracane rossastro;* rocchio of *Porf. bigio.* XIII., *Four cols spirally moulded *Pav.* XIV., floor of Mosaic scraps, *Palombino latteo.* XV., 942 Sarcophagus in *Pario.* XVI., small bronze Venus on pedestal of *Rosso di Levanto.*

In corridor on 1st floor, Compartment X., above Sarcophagus, inscribed slab of *Cip. rosso br.*

Museo Archeologico.—Broken col of *Br. della Villa Casali.* Good specimens of *Br. dor., Br. di Aleppo, Br. pav. min.,* and *Br. di Simone; Cottanello antico pav.; Cip. mand. lionato; Affr. bigio fiorito; Occhio di Pav. pav.; Settebasi dor.; Bianco e Nero tigrato*; *Al. bianco ondato* and *Pecorella ; Porf. bigio, Porf. nero, Porf. verde* and *Porf. serp. nero ; Gr. della Sedia.*

Museo Capitolino.

COURT.—In rt. corner, col of *Cip. ondato.*

ATRIUM: 39 fragment of colossal Statue, *Porf. rosso lattinato* B.

ROOM TO RT.—8 bust of woman on pedestal of *Br. gialla e pav.* Two lions in *Gr. nero,* partly spotted behind with *Gr. brecciato* B. Isis in *Gr. nero* S (*tigrato*).

6 fragment of kneeling Egyptian statue, *Basalte bigio*.

GALLERIA.—5 Cupid in *Tirio ;* 7 Male Bust in *Tirio ;* 9 Boy's head in *Lunense ;* 14 Vase in *Pario ;* 31, 32 Rocchi in *Gr. di Elba.*

57 Pedestal, *P. santa fiorita ;* 64 female bust on plinth of *Affr. principe ;* plinth of busts 56-60, 62-66, *Nero antico* C.

SALA DELLE COLOMBE. 42 Chimera, *Al. a rosa* (*list.*) S.

55 Pedestal, *Diaspro di Siracusa.*
61 Left breast of bust, *Lum. bigia di Egitto* S. Pedestal, *P. santa violetta.*
Disk below sarcophagus, **Br*. *verde di Egitto.*
Venus in *Lesbio* C (*Pario gialloguolo* B).
SALA DEGL' IMPERATORI. 1 Bust of *Al. tartaruga* C.
4 Pedestal of Tiberius, *Porto Venere.*
31 Bust of Hadrian, *Al. verdognolo cupo* B; 33 Bust of Giulia Sabina, *Cotognino verdiccio;* 51 Bust of Sept. Severus. *Al. verdognolo chiaro* B (*gialloguolo*) S.
56 Bust, *Al. agatato.*
65 Bust of Giordano Giovine, *Lum. orientale bigia di Egitto* R.
Door-jambs between Gladiator and Faun, and between Emperors and Philosophers, *Br. gialla fibrosa* B.
SALONE. Door-jambs of *Cottanello antico.*
Jupiter and two Centaurs, *Bigio morato lumachellato.*
Colossal Boy Hercules, *Basalte verde.*
Statue of Aesculapius, *Nero bigiastro* B.
Two inter. cols *P. santa* C.
25 Colossal bust of Antoninus Pius, *Luneuse.*
Faun, *Rosso antico* (*striato*) B.
SALA DEL GLADIATORE.
3, 5 Rocchi of *Settebasi bigia giallastra.*
11 Col of *Al. a giaccione* S.
13 Col of **Br*. *traccagnina fior.*
Museo delle Terme.—In the Cloister: I., 37 Rocchio of *Fiore di Persico ven.* II., 16, 18 *Porto Venere schizzato;* 40 *Cor. rosea.* IV., in the centre, two cols *Porf. bigio;* 37 Rocchio of **Porta Santa bigia br.;* 39 *Giallo carnagione.* In the Garden, *Bath of *Porf. nero;* round basin of *Gr. rosso min.*
Room I., 11 Rocchio of *Bigio chiaro.* II., 7 *Porf. bigio.* IV., Plinth of *Porta Santa br. min.* VI., Rocchio of *Trac. rossa lum.* VII., 4 Rocchio of *Rosso di Levanto;* 8 Bust of *Lum. bigia di Egitto.* VIII., 10 Rocchio of *Broccatellone chiaro.* X., Girl's head in *Pentelico.* XI., 13 Rocchio of *Br. di S. Ipolito.*

Museo Torlonia.
125 Bust on rocchio of *Serravezza antica*.
189 Bust on rocchio of *Affr. verde*.
383 Plinth of *Affr. principe*.
384 Bath of *Bianco e nero tigrato*.
388 Fluted and moulded cols of *Pav. argentino* and *Pav. bianco*.
397 Rocchio of *Cip. prasio*.
399, 403 Rocchi of *Settebasi bianca*.
400 Rocchio of *Astracane rossastro*.
426 Two wild boars in *Bigio mor*.
443 Large col of *Sard. a rosa*.
506 Large tazza of *Br. verde di Egitto*.

Obelisks.
Lateran, *Gr. rosco* R.
Minerva, *Gr. rosso delle Guglie* B (*rosco* R).
Monte Cavallo, *Gr. roseo*.
Monte Citorio, *Gr. rosso*, with four restored slabs of *Gr. rosso macchiato* B.
Pantheon, *Gr. rosso* B.
Piazza Navona, *Gr. rosso* B.
Piazza del Popolo, *Gr. rosso*.
Piazza dei Termini, *Gr. rosco*.
Pincio, *Gr. rosso* B.
S. M. Maggiore, *Gr. roseo*.
Trinità dei Monti, *Gr. rosso*.
Vatican, *Gr. rosso delle Guglie* B (*roseo* R).
Villa Mattei, *Gr. rosso delle Guglie* B.

Pal. Altemps.
CHAPEL.—Vertical strips on walls, *Br. dor. pav.*
Three cols *Pav.*; one *Settebasi bruna giallastra*; two *Broccatellone rosso*; urn, *Giallo br.*
Oval below window *Pav. br. fior.*; jambs of doors, *Rosso br. confuso*.

Pal. Altieri.
Two cols *Porf. rosso* C; two *Al. a giaccione* C.

Pal. Barberini.
Two fluted cols *Pav.*; two cols *Al. gialloguolo*; *two *Bianco e nero antico* C.

Pal. Borghese.—Two cols *Cor.* C.

Pal. Braschi.

Fourteen cols in portico and Court, *Cip. verde.*
Pilasters of staircase, *Settebasi venata* S.
Round slabs on each landing, *Rosso br. minuto* S.

Pal. Bufalo.—Two small cols above door, *Cip.*

Pal. della Camera.

In loggia, overlooking fountain, two cols *Bigio br.*; one *Bigio lum.*; two *Cor.*; two *Br. rossa* : two *Cip. verde chiaro*; five *Bigio antico.*

Pal. Colonna.

Inner court, *Col of *Cip. verde* C.
Ground floor, two cols *Pav.*; two engrailed *Rosso antico*; two cols *Verde antico*; two *Giallo antico*; spiral col of *Rosso striato.*
In gallery, two cols *Verde antico*; two fluted cols *Giallo antico.*

Pal. dei Conservatori.

In Court, col of *Porf. rosso* C; two cols *F. di Persico.*
Room V., *Rocchio of *Br. verde di Egitto* B (*porfiroide* R).
Little she-wolf—relief, *Lum. gialla min.* B (*bigiastra*).
Two cols *Verde antico* C.
In Sculpture room, Dog in *V. ran. lineare*; 81 fluted *rocchio of *Pav. cupo reticolato.*
At foot of stairs leading to Pinacoteca, broken rocchio of *Br. frutticolosa min.*

Pal. Doria.

At bottom of stairs, two cols *Tasio* C.
†Two cols *Cip. mand. rosso* R.
†Spiral col *Bigio morato*; two cols *Nero antico.*
*†Two cols *Br. policroma* B (*Trac. disfatta*); four cols *Verde antico.*
Large vase of *Al. rossastro ven.*
Bacchus in *Rosso antico.*
Vase of *Porf. rosso.*
Two cols *Bigio dislocato*; two *Verde chiaro.*
†Recumbent Nile in *Basalte bruno.*
†Two cols *P. santa,* and two in the Chapel.

† In private rooms.

Cols in pairs at upper windows facing the Corso; N. *Br. di Serravezza;* S. *Serravezza macchiata.*
At doorways, N. *Cip. verde* and *Bigio cip.*; S. *Cip. zonale* and *C. verde.*

Pal. Farnese.
In Court, *two cols *Gr. bigio bronzato*; at loggia, above entrance, four cols *Verde antico.*

Pal. Grazioli (Rte. 3).—At doorway, two *cols *Gr. bigio minuto rossastro.*

Pal. Maccarani (Via dell' Umiltà), two cols *Gr. del Foro* at door.

Pal. Madama.—Door-jambs on 1st floor, especially 1st rt., *Giallo carnagione tigrato* B.

Pal. Massimi (alle Colonne).
In Chapel, two cols *Cip.*; two *Br. pav.*; four *Bigio antico.*

Pal. di Papa Giulio.
Front of *Peperino*; two three-quarter cols *Gr. persichino*; two fountain basins of *Gr. del Foro* C.
In loggia, col of *P. santa*, col of *Pentelico.*

Pal. Quirinale.
Two cols *P. santa* C; two *Occhio di Pav. rosso* S; two *Occhio di Pav. pav.* C.
In Chapel, on screen, eight short cols *P. santa.*
In garden, five cols *Tirio* C.

Pal. Rospigliosi.
On ground floor, *large col of *F. di Persico rosso* R; *tazza of *Verde antico sanguigno* B (*rubiginoso* R); col of *P. santa*; col of *Verde antico*; two cols *Bigio mor.*
In Casino, two large cols *Rosso antico* B (*striato*); four *Cor. pall.*; all cut in half by a wall.

Pal. Sciarra.
[On ground floor, two large *cols *Lum. rosea* B (*Astracane madreperlifero* R); two *Al.*; one *Giallo antico*; one *Verde antico*; two Egyptian statues in *Gr. nero* C.]

Pal. del Senatore.—Two cols *P. santa* C.

Pal. Spada.—Two cols *P. santa* C.

Pal. Torlonia (Corso).

Six cols *Cor. di Cori*: six *Gr. bigio*: four *Gr. persichino*. In private rooms: two *P. santa*: four *Palombara*; two *Broccatellone*: one *Porf. rosso* C. Two bacchanti in *Bigio morato*. Vase of *Br. trac. fior.* Recumbent Nile in *Basalte bruno* C.

Pal. Torlonia (al Borgo).

In portico, col of *Pav.*: col of *Bigio mor.* C.

Pal. Valentini.—On ground floor, ten cols *Pav.*: one *Bigio mor.*: underground, five cols *Gr. bianco e nero* C.

Piazza Colonna.—Twelve fluted *cols, and two pilasters, of *Tasio* C; large bath of *P. santa*.

Piazza Branca (S. M. del Pianto).—*Col of *Porf. bigio*.

Piazza S. M. Maggiore.—Large fluted col of *Imezio*.

Piazza di Pietra.—Eleven cols *Lunense*.

Piazza Rondinini.—Two cols *Porino* in court of No. 48.

Piazza di Spagna.—Obelisk of *Cip. verde giallastro* R, with panels of *Serravezza pav.* (resembling *Affricano*).

Pincio.

Outside the gate, fountain basin of *Lesbio*: at the curved terrace, three cols *Gr. del Foro*.

Porta del Popolo.—Two cols *Pav. br.*; four *Gr. del Sempione*.

Porticus of Octavia.—Four fluted cols *Pario* C.

Pyramid of Cestius.—Covered with *Tasio* C.

Scuola Castigliana.—On the left, two colonnettes, *Taormina*; at the curtain, two of *Al. list.* C. (*verdiccio*); four cols *Br. pav.*; two colonnettes, *Diaspro giallo*.

Scuola Siciliana.—Two cols at the curtain, in very bad light, left, *Settebasi gatteggiante*; rt., *Pav. br.*

Sepolcro dei Nasoni.—Interior of *Tufo lionato* B.

Tarpeian Rock.—*Tufo rosso* B.

Theatre of Marcellus.—*Travertino di Tivoli* B.

University.—At Library door, two cols *Occhio di Pav. pav.* S.

VATICAN.

Sala Regia.—Two cols *Br. pav.* C; four large slabs in a row on wall opposite Sistine Chapel, *P. santa ranciata* B.

Cappella Paolina.—Two cols *Pav.* C.

Appartamenti Borgia.—Three cols *Cor.*; four *Br. pav.*; two *Pav.*; two *Imezio* C.

Four large cols *Bardiglio dor.* R; two cols *Bigio mor.* B (*ven.*).

Large tazza of *F. di Persico* (*reticolare* S, *muscoloso* R); tripod of *Pav.* C.

Library.

Two cols *Occhio di Pav. pav. scuro* R; six cols *Porf. rosso pomato*; four *Giallo antico*; spiral col *Cotognino bianco*.

Cameo of Octavius Augustus, *Agata cotognina* C.

Candlebearer of *Cristallo iridato*; lenzuolo of *Amianto* C; four tables of *Labradore*; two cols at door, *Al. fior.*

Scala Nobile.—Six cols *Gr. bigio*; five *Gr. persichino*; four *Gr. rosso*; three *Gr. del Foro*.

At the first landing, *four cols *Cor. carnina ven.*; higher up, four cols *Cor. di Cori*.

Overlooking Croce Greca, *two cols *Porfido nero* B (see p. 195).

Croce Greca.

Sphinxes, rt. *Gr. rosso pall.*, l. *Gr. bigio rossastro*; two large Sarcophagi, *Porf. rosso porporino*; strips on pavement and circle round mosaic, *Cip. rosso macchiato* B.

Sala della Biga.

Four rings on pavement, *Cip. rosso macchiato* B.

Chariot in *Lunense antico*.

613 Sarcophagus in *Tirio*.

Candelabri.

Eight cols (most of them much broken), *Bigio antico*; [on the left, *B. lum. chiaro, B. cip. dor., B. chiaro, B. ven.*; rt., *B. ossifero chiaro, B. chiaro dor., B. lum. chiaro, B. bicolore*].

Four cols of *Al. di Civitavecchia*.

1 *Vase of *Br. verde di Egitto*, on rocchio of *Porf. rosso ubbriaco* (*chiaro*).

14 Two-handled vase of *Porf. rosso porporino*; on rocchio of *Gr. bigio cupo tigrato*. 17, 18 Vases of *Gr. bigio e nero*.

21 Vase of *Pentelico* on rocchio of *Verde pall.*

31 Candlebearer in *Pentelico*.
33 Bowl of *Gr. bigio macchiato*; on rocchio of *Cip. verde increspato* B.
46 *Two-handled vase of *Serp. bigia verdastra*; on rocchio of *Gr. bigio min. lineare.*
56 Vase of *Serp. verde e pav.* on rocchio of *Porf. bigio rossastro* B.
48 Vase of *Gr. bigio dend.*; on rocchio of *Giallo br.*
50 *Vase of *Porf. serp. bigio* R. (crowded with chips).
52 Recumbent Bacchus in *Basalte bronzino*; head and rt. arm restored in *B. verde* B.
69 *Vase of *Diaspro Lisimaco*; on rocchio of *Br. di Aleppo* B.
70, 123 Two vases of *Porf. serp. nero* B; on rocchi of *Gr. rosso* and *Bardiglio*.
79 Funeral urn of *Lunense antico*.
On sarcophagus 83, two vases of *Serp. bigia di Ponsevera*.
83D Vase of *Cotognino bianco ven.* S.
87 Statuette in *Lesbio*, bearing vase of *Bigio turc.*
95 Vase of *Serp. di Genova* (*bigia verdastra*).
96 Vase of *Serp. di Tebe* (*pav. verdastra*).
98 Colossal foot of *Al. apennino dorato* R.
100 Funeral urn in *Lunense macchiato*.
113B Vase of *Gr.* (*Serp.*) *di Genova*.
113C Tazza of *Giallo tigrato pall.*
113D Vase of *Serp. pav. di Ponsevera*.
120 Flat tazza of *Al. giallo fior.*; on tripod of *Al. a rosa sfrangiato* B.
159 Vase of *Br. verde di Genova* on *Al. ghiacciolo rossastro*.
163 Small Silenus on plinth of *Pav. br. argentino*.
166 Small Candlebearer in *Pentelico* on base of *Gr. bianco e nero*.
171 Cinerary Vase of *Al. bianco*; 173C fluted rocchio of *Palombino bianco*.
175, 179 Vases of *Lunense antico*.
181 Channelled tazza of *Rosso striato* on col of *Bigio chiaro*.
181, 196 *Channelled foot of *Lum. rossa min.*; 185 Vase of *Verde ran. maculato* B.
188 Vase of *Al. di Orte* on rocchio of *Cip. marino min.*, with lower plinth of *Affr. violetto ven.*

189 Vase of *Diaspro rosso ven.*; on rocchio of *Giallo carnagione.*
191 Vase of *Nero antico* on pedestal of *Gr. di Genova.*
202, 206 Vases of *Al. onichino* and *Cotognino arancio list.*
204 Behind sarcophagus, half buried in the wall, Vase of *Al. onichino rossastro.*
204A Vase of *Al. melleo list.*; 204C *Al. list.*
212 Channelled vase and rocchio of *Tirio.*
213 Boy with bird, *Pario.*
217 Vase of *Gr. rossastro tigrato.*
225 Vase of *Palombino bianco*; 228 Vase of *Al. bruno rossastro list.*
235, 236 Two large Vases, *Serp. granatifera* B.
239 Tazza of *Porf. serp. verde agatato* B; on plinth of *Diaspro rosso e verde.*
243 Boy with cock and jug, in *Tirio.*
247 Tazza of *Gr. rosso min. (roseo min.* B).
249 Tazza of *Porf. verde.*
221 Vase of *Rosso antico* on foot of *Lum. rossa min.*, and plinth of *Rosso br.*
268 *Little vase of *Gr. bigio grafico* on rocchio of *Gr. bigio verdognolo* B (*pedicolare* R).
269 Fallen warrior in *Lunense macchiato*, and statuette of *Pentelico.*
606 Four-handled vase of *Gr. verde bronzato* B (between cols of *Porf. nero.*).

Arazzi.
Four cols *Porf. rosso* (from S. Bartolommeo); four *Verde antico.*

Sala Rotonda.—Large tazza of *Porf. rosso*; pedestals of statues, *Imezio fasciato schietto.*

Sala delle Muse.—Sixteen cols *Bardiglio ven. chiaro* from Hadrian's Villa.

Sala degli Animali.—176 Col of *Al. fior.*
177 Engrailed col of *Lesbio* S.
103 Griffin in *Sard. tartarugato giallo* B (*bruno*).
112 Stork in *Rosso antico.*
119 Dog in *Pav. bianco* on stand of *Pav. bigio verdognolo br.*
132 Stag in *Al. fior.* S (*rosso macchiato* R) on base of *Verde di Susa* (showing contrast with 244).

133 *Lion in *G. eburneo* br. R restored in *Giallo carnagione* S; on base of *Gr. verde plasmato* B (*min.* R).
135 Crawfish in *Verde di Prato*.
247 Tazza of *Pav. br.*
149 *Lion in *Giallo br.*
155, 163 Small panthers in *Gr. tigrato bianco* B.
156 *Lion in *Bigio perlato* R (*Bardiglio scuro* B).
168 Porpoise in *Porf. serp. verde*.
190 Slab of *Pav. br. min.*
195 Lion tearing horse, *Tirio*.
Tazza of *Verde ran. ond.* B ; three feet sustaining it, *V. r. fibroso* R.
229 Crab in *Porf. verde* B.
244, 245 *Two tables, *Verde principe*.

Galleria delle Statue.

Splayed pilasters of *Settebasi gialla* S.
Beside Ariadne (412), *Cor. violacea* B (*carnina ven.* R).
271, 390 Sitting statues in *Lesbio*.
250 Cupid in *Tirio*.
421 Vase of *Al. orientale agatino* on base of *Verde chiaro*.
133 *Col of *Al. fior. list.*, on base of *Settebasi pav.*
398 Large Bath of *Cotognino orientale ven.* (*Al. bianco pom.*).

Sala dei Busti.

278 Cloak of *Al. verdognolo* S.
293 Spiral rocchio of *Nero antico* ; upon it, mask in *Rosso antico*.
298 Jupiter Serapis, in *Basalte bruno* (*bronzino*) S.
339 Oval vase of *Affr. fior.* on base of *P. santa alabastrina*.
340 Oval vase, *Al. di Civitavecchia*, on base of *Al. a giaccione*.
389 Fragment of *Al. di Orte*.

Gabinetto delle Maschere.—Outside, Vase of *Serp. di Genova fior.* on rocchio of *Settebasi dor.*

Eight cols *Al. del Monte Circeo*.
425 Dancing girl in *Lesbio*.
432, 435 Unpolished Faun and tazza, *Rosso antico porfidino* B.
438 Chair of *Rosso antico* on base of *Br. bianca e nera*.
443 Apollo in *Porino*.

Octagon.

25 Col of *Porf. bigio* B.

26, 102 Sculptured cols of *Pentelico*.
29 Large Bath of *Gr. nero* B (*min.* R).
31A, 97A *Cols of *Cor. gialla*.
36 Small oblong bath of *Gr. nero verdastro*.
40 Rocchio of *Affr. verde picchiettato* R ; central part, *Affr. cor. zonale* B.
41, 46 Two fragments of moulded cornice in *Rosso antico*.
43 *Bath of *P. santa ven. a Stuoia*.
45A, 87D *Cols of *Bigio reticolato*.
50 Rocchio of *Porf. pav. pomato*.
62, 89 Large Baths of *Gr. rosso*.
71B Col of *Lunense antico*.
82 Bath of *Gr. del Foro* S.
84 Two masses of *Al. a pecorella carnino* B (*dor.*).
85 Goddess in *Pario*.
92 Apollo di Belvedere in *Lunense antico* B.
100 *Bath of *Basalte verde* B.
101 *Col of *Porf. rosso pomato*.

Belvedere.
Tazza of *Pav. ad inchiostro* : Meleager in *Tirio* R.
Sarcophagus of Scipio Barbatus, *Peperino* B; Torso in *Porino*.

Museo Chiaramonti.
589 Statue of Mercury in *Lesbio*.
464 Mithraic sacrifice, in *Bigio mor.*
463 Pig in *Nero antico*.
460 Fragment of draped statue, *Al. ven.* S.
315 Leopard in *Gr. tigrato*.
314 Slab of *Pav. verdiccio*.
6, 13 Slabs of *Scrp. reticolata di Elba*.
Two cols at gate, *Bigio macchiato nerastro* S.

Gallery of Inscriptions.
XXXVIII., To rt. of Library door, third stone from the top, *Lum. persichina* B.
XXVI., l. of window, oblong inscribed Victoria Filie, *Br. pav. reticolata* S.
Slab inscribed Ulpia Decorata, *Cip. verde increspato* B.

Many sepulchral slabs in *Bigio ven. scuro* B, and many in *Greco br. scuro* R.

Braccio Nuovo.

*Eight cols *Cip. bigio e nero* B; *two cols *Gr. nero tigrato*; two cols *Al. bianco* C; two cols *Giallo rossastro*.
Eight slabs on pavement under dome, *Bianco e nero di Francia* B.
39 Bacchic Vase, *Basalte bruno*.
45 Bust of *Al. a giaccione*.
53 Euripides, *Tasio* C.
87 Bust, *Al. verdognolo chiaro* B.
114 Statue of Minerva in *Pario giallognolo*.
Pavement between 92-41, and 111-26, *Settebasi poligonia* B.
Col on rt. in Exedra, *Gr. persichino min.* S.
Five slabs on pavement, *P. santa madreporitica* B.
Between Braccio Nuovo and M. Chiaramonti, two cols *Gr. del Foro* on plinth of *Cip. bigio rigato*.

Etruscan Museum.

In hemicycle, 103 *Rocchio of *Al. fior. pav.*; several rocchi of *Gr. bigio min.* in various shades.
In room of Vases, rocchi of *Cip. bigiastro* and *Gr. persichino*.

Egyptian Museum.

2 Large sarcophagus of *Basalte bronzino* B; 5 *Basalte nero*.
11 Idol of *Arenaria gialla di Egitto* B.
13 Idol of *Arenaria rossa di Egitto* B.
26 Sitting statue of *Gr. tigrato verdognolo* B.
17 Colossal statue with feet restored in another granite, *Gr. tigrato verde* B.
Two lions with hieroglyphics, *Gr. bigio min.* B (*rossiccio* R).
12, 14 Two colossal statues, *Gr. rosso verdognolo* B.
23 Fragment of statue, *Al. di Karnak*.
19 Fragment of kneeling man, almost life size, *Basalte verde* B.
25 Torso of *Gr. nero rossastro min.* 27 Colossal Nile in *Bigio mor.*
44, 51 Two statues of Isis, and (112) kneeling idol, *Gr. nero br.* B.
28 Osiride, in *Gr. nero tigrato*.

29 Statuette in *Verde ran. orbicolare*, restored in *Verde ran. linearc.*
34 *Idol of *Semesanto pav. pall.*
121 Crocodile in *Basaltc verde* B.
36 Antinous in *Lunense antico* B.
38 Statue of Isis, in *Palombino bruniccio* B.
62 Apis, *Gr. nero* B.
39 Idol in *Gr. bigio turc.*
41, 43 Pedestal of Sphinxes, *Verde ran. giallastro.*
45 Crocodile in *Pentelico.*
46 Double hermes of Isis and Apis, and of Isis and Tau, *Bianco e nero di Egitto* B.
53 Crocodile in *Paragone.*
Isis and Horus, *Gr. bigio turc.*
Sitting statuette, *Gr. nero.*
87 Table in *Al. di Karnak.*
HEMICYCLE.—147 colossal statue, *Gr. tigrato verdognolo* B.
Three standing statues, *Gr. tigrato rosso* B.
Two large mummy cases, with hieroglyphics, *Palombino giallo-gnolo lum.* B (one unpolished); many stelae of *Arenaria rossa e gialla.*
134 Pedestal of *Br. verde di Egitto.*
Canopo di stela, *Calcarea gialliccia di Egitto* B.

Garden.

CASINO of Pius IV.—Four fluted cols *Giallo antico* C.
NICCHIONE.—Two cols *Pav.*; *two *Basaltc verde*; eight *Bigio lum.*; one *Imezio*; one *Tirio* C.

Via del Cardello.—Two cols *Porta santa* in Court at No. 15.
Villa Albani.
Many beautiful cols of *Gr. bigio* and *Gr. persichino*; two cols *Br. pav. rossastra*; col of *Bigio dislocato.*
37 Tazza of *Lunense macchiato*; bust of Berenice, *Porf. bigio turc.* R.
2nd GALLERY.—Two cols *Bigio ven.* (one on rt. very beautiful).
ROOM VIII. (outside at door), two cols *Gr. nero*; *col of *Greco scritto.*

Large inter. col of *Al. fior.* B (partly *br.*; at base, *mellco*; in the centre, *giallognolo* S).

*Door-jambs of *Cip. verde rigato*; col of *Bigio scritto.*
160 Mithraic priest, *Affr. pav.*
1st CABINET.—Colossal bust in *Basalte nero* C.
3rd CABINET.—Two cols *Tirio.*
CHAPEL.—Four cols *Occhio di Pav. rosso* C.
BILLIARD ROOM.—Two cols *Lesbio* B; two cols and vase of *Br. di Egitto scura* R.
654 Head of lion, *Basalte verde.*
660 Female bust, *Pario*, on pedestal of *Semesantone rosso.*
665 Foot of pedestal, *Gr. verde ad Erbetta.*
675 Moulded base in *Pav. verde.*
679 Col of *Verde di Ponsevera.*
692 Rocchio of *Occhio di Pav. pav. piccolo.*
TEMPIETTO.—Four fluted cols *Bigio antico* C.
FIRST FLOOR.—Pilasters of *F. di Persico reticolare* S (*ad inchiostro*); lower part of pilasters, especially mouldings, *Settebasi gatt.* S.
Walls and side jambs of windows, *Greco ven.* S.
Two tables of *Br. verde di Egitto.*
Vase on rocchio of *Porf. rosso laterizio* R.
930 Vase of *Br. di Svezia.*
932 *Vase of *Gr. verde ad erbetta.*
934 Bust of Annius Verus, *Al. biancastro.*
964 Pedestal of Aesop, *Giallo di Siena.*
966 Bust of Pius V., *P. santa lum.*
994 Colossal Antinous in *Lunense antico.*
*Door-jambs of *Pav. bigio br. argentino.*
Door-jambs of *Settebasi biancastra* S.
1000 Vase of *Porf. verde dor.*
ROOM OF PARNASSUS, *Cip. marino violetto* S; foliage of pilasters *Verde di Firenze* S.
1031 Fireplace below relief, *Giallo carnagione.*

Villa Borghese.

CHAPEL (overlooking sunken lawn). Lower part of 2nd col, left, in portico, *Cip. prasio* B.

CASINO.—In portico, two cols *Lum. bruna rossastra;* two *Lum. bigia giallastra;* 23 col of *Gr. del Foro arrugginito.*
Plinth below busts and statues in entrance hall, *Affr. principe S.
Eight cols *Gr. rossastro del Sempione:* specchi of *Br. di S. Ipolito.*
III., 62 Leda in *Pario:* 103 standing boy, *Pentelico;* boy's head (19), *Lunense.*
101 Vase of *Al. melleo'list.*
VI., Two cols *Cotognino bianco list.* S; *Vase of *Gr. verde min.* B; sleeping boy and two oblong vases in *Paragone.*
Legs of two tables, *Al. di Montauto.*
VII., 173 Vase of *Al. tartaruga giallastro.*
Two cols *Giallo antico* C, on plinth of *Br. di Aleppo.*
Under Thorn boy, plinth of *Br. trac.;* two cols *Porf. rosso (pav.).*
VIII., Four cols *Cor. di Cori;* below six statues, *Cor. pav. scura.*
*Two cols *Pav. br.* C; on plinth of *Serravezza pav.*
Under two tables, dolphins in *Al. a Montauto.*
IX., In corners, four Vases of *Al. a giaccione.*
17 *Al. rosso* on plinth of *Porf. verde.*
24 *Al. a rosa.*
X., Tazza of *Rosso antico* C, on plinth of *Porf. verde.*
Two sphinxes, *Basalte verde* C.
Several oval basins of *Bianco e nero tigrato* S (*granitoide* R).
204 Tazza of *Gr. bianco e nero* on rocchio of *Bianco e nero tigrato,* showing contrast. The latter is pinkish, and is marked in pools.
208 Tazza of *Gr. bigio verdastro.*
210 Tazza of *Cor. nuv.*
209 Draped Statue in *Nero antico* C.
Two colonnettes at altar, beside statue 216, *Gr. bigio perlato* B.
119 Two four-handled vases, *Al. giallo list.*
Tazza of *Cor. min. nuv.*
220, 222 Cylindrical vases of *Cotognino list.*
Vase of *Al. fior.*
36 *Cotognino cupo.*

Villa Ludovisi.
Large tazza of *Verde ran. chiaro.*
Mask of *Rosso antico* C.
Spirally fluted *col of *Pav. br. dor.*

Villa Mattei.
Obelisk of *Gr. rosso delle Guglie* B.
In front of Casino, *two rocchi *Br. gialla* B.
*Col of *Affr. ven.* C.
Statue of *Giallo antico* C.

Villa Torlonia.
*Four cols *Cor.* C ; two obelisks in *Gr. del Sempione* C.

INDEX.

Showing the true *Genera* and *Species*. All other marbles are *Varieties*, frequently occurring together on the same large slab or column.

Affricano bigio, 99.
„ nero, 100.
„ rosso, 101.
„ verde, 102.
Agate, 120.
Alabastro ametista, 103.
„ bianco, 103.
„ bruno, 104.
„ di Civitavecchia, 111.
„ cotognino, 112.
„ fiorito, 105.
„ fortezzino, 106.
„ a giaccione, 106.
„ giallo, 107.
„ di Karnak, 111.
„ listato, 107.
„ marino, 107.
„ melleo, 107.
„ di Montauto, 111.
„ di Monte Circeo, 112.
„ a nuvole, 108.
„ occhiuto, 108.
„ onichino, 108.
„ di Orte, 112.
„ di Palombara, 113.

Alabastro a Pecorella, 116.
„ pomato, 109.
„ a Rosa, 109.
„ rosso, 110.
„ Sardonico, 114.
„ a tartaruga, 116.
„ verdognolo, 111.
Amianto, 128.
Arenaria, 122.
Bardiglio, 54.
Basalt, 139.
Bianco e Giallo, 68.
Bianco e Nero antico, 47.
„ di Egitto, 47.
„ di Francia, 48.
„ di Perugia, 48.
„ di Porto Ferrajo, 48.
„ tigrato, 47.
Bigio antico, 49.
„ lumacato, 51.
„ morato, 53.
Breccia di Aleppo, 81.
„ bianca e nera, 81.
„ corallina, 89.
„ „ di Cori, 89.

Breccia dorata, 81.
„ frutticolosa, 82.
„ gialla, 82.
„ Gregoriana, 83.
„ pavonazza, 83.
„ Quintilina, 85.
„ rossa, 85.
„ di S. Ipolito, 86.
„ a Semesanto, 94.
„ di Serravezza, 87.
„ di Settebasi, 92.
„ di Simone, 88.
„ di Svezia, 88.
„ traccagnina, 95.
„ verde, 88.
„ verde di Egitto, 88.
„ della Villa Casali, 81.
Broccatello, 78.
Broccatellone, 98.
Calcarea, 122.
Cipollino bigio, 61.
„ mandolato, 62.
„ nero, 61.
„ rosso, 61.
„ verde, 59.
Cottanello, 63.
Diaspro, 118.
„ di Sicilia, 119.
Fiore di Persico, 64.
Giallo antico, 54.
„ di Siena, 57.
„ tigrato, 57.
Giallo e Nero, 58.
Granito bianco e nero, 137.
„ bigio, 134.

Granito della Colonna, 138.
„ dendritico, 138.
„ di Elba, 139.
„ del Foro, 133.
„ di Giglio, 136.
„ nero, 137.
„ persichino, 136.
„ rosso, 132.
„ della Sedia, 138.
„ del Sempione, 139.
„ tigrato, 136.
„ verde, 138.
Greco, 46.
Imezio, 44.
Labrador, 120.
Lapis lazzuli, 120.
Legno pietrificato, 119.
Lesbio, 43.
Lumachella degli Abruzzi, 75.
„ di Astracane, 78.
„ bigia, 75.
„ di Calabria, 76.
„ gialla, 76.
„ nera, 77.
„ pavonazza, 77.
„ rossa, 77.
Luñense (Carrara), 44.
Malachite, 121.
Manziana, 142.
Nero antico, 48.
Occhio di Pavone, 79.
„ „ Pernice, 99.
Palombino, 45.
Paragone, 140.
Pario, 42.

Pavonazzetto, 65.
Pentelico, 42.
Peperino, 142.
Pietra Nefritica, 127.
Plasma di Smeraldo, 121.
Porfido bigio, 130.
„ nero, 130.
„ rosso, 128.
„ verde, 129.
Porfido Serpentino bigio, 131.
„ „ nero, 131.
„ „ verde, 131.
Porino, 42.
Porta Santa, 69.
Porto Venere, 58.
Rosso antico, 59.
„ brecciato, 97.
„ di Francia, 74.
„ di Lēvănto, 124.

Selce, 141.
Serpentina comune, 122.
„ dell' Elba, 123.
„ di Genova, 123.
„ di Tebe, 123.
Spato fluore, 121.
Sperone, 142.
Taormina, 74.
Tasio, 43.
Tirio, 44.
Travertine, 141.
Tufa, 143.
Verde antico, 125.
„ di Firenze, 127.
„ di Grecia, 127.
„ di Ponsēvĕra, 123.
„ di Prato, 125.
„ ranocchia, 124.
„ di Susa, 127.

www.ingramcontent.com/pod-product-compliance
Lightning Source LLC
Chambersburg PA
CBHW020832230426
43666CB00007B/1200